PRESENTED TO:

_____

FROM:

_____

ANITA CORRINE DONIHUE

When I'm

PRAISING
GOD

DEVOTIONAL THOUGHTS ON
WORSHIP FOR WOMEN

BARBOUR

© MCMXCIX by Barbour Publishing, Inc.

ISBN 1-59310-035-3

Designed by UDG | DesignWorks, Sisters, Oregon

Published by Barbour Publishing, Inc., P.O. Box 719, Uhrichsville, Ohio 44683   www.barbourbooks.com

 Member of the
Evangelical Christian
Publishers Association

Printed in China.

5 4 3 2 1

Special thanks to my dear teacher,

mentor, and friend,

COLLEEN L. REECE,

for her dedicated teaching, help,

and encouragement through the years.

CONTENTS

GRATITUDE

My God, how endless is Thy love!
Thy gifts are ev'ry evening new;
And morning mercies from above
Gently distill like early dew.

Thou spread'st the curtains of the night
Great Guardian of my sleeping hours;
Thy sov'reign word restores the light
And quickens all my drowsy pow'rs.

I yield my pow'rs to Thy command.
To Thee I consecrate my days;
Perpetual blessings from Thy hand
Demand perpetual songs of praise.

ISAAC WATTS

It is good to praise the Lord and make music to your name, O Most High, to proclaim your love in the morning and your faithfulness at night.

PSALM 92:1–2 NIV

Armor of God

Finally, be strong in the Lord and in his mighty power. Put on the full armor of God so that you can take your stand against the devil's schemes. For our struggle is not against flesh and blood, but against the rulers, against the authorities, against the powers of this dark world and against the spiritual forces of evil in the heavenly realms. Therefore put on the full armor of God, so that when the day of evil comes, you may be able to stand your ground, and after you have done everything, to stand. Stand firm then, with the belt of truth buckled around your waist, with the breastplate of righteousness in place, and with your feet fitted with the readiness that comes from the gospel of peace. In addition to all this, take up the shield of faith, with which you can extinguish all the flaming arrows of the evil one. Take the helmet of salvation and the sword of the Spirit, which is the word of God. And pray in the Spirit on all occasions with all kinds of prayers and requests. With this in mind, be alert and always keep on praying for all the saints.

EPHESIANS 6:10–18 NIV

Everyone felt afraid of the Philistine giant, Goliath. He towered over nine feet tall. He wore a bronze helmet, bronze leg plates, and a bronze javelin was strapped to his back. In his huge hand he carried a spear. The point alone possibly weighed about twenty pounds. His shield bearer walked or ran before him.

"Come here," he said, "and I'll give your flesh to the birds of the air and the beasts of the field!"

David said to the Philistine, "You come against me with sword and spear and javelin, but I come against you in the name of the LORD Almighty, the God of the armies of Israel, whom you have defied."

1 SAMUEL 17:44–45 NIV

Before this, young David had taken his staff in hand, stooped down, and picked up five smooth stones and placed them in the pouch of his bag. Shepherd's staff in one hand and a sling in the other, he approached the giant. We all know how this victorious story ended.

Eileen loved to roller-blade. She kept up with the best of them. For Christmas and birthdays she had received all the proper gear from her parents in order to blade safely: a helmet and shoulder, elbow, wrist, knee, and shin guards. Her family made sure that she had all the necessities. They knew what could happen.

One nice afternoon Eileen had a half hour free. In a hurry, she grabbed all her gear except the wrist guards that had fallen in the corner.

It wasn't long until Eileen hit a curb wrong and went flying. Sure enough, she broke her wrist.

It's the same way with our armor from God. We can't live victorious lives unless we put on all His armor. It won't work with everything but faith. Neither will we see victory in Jesus without knowing or telling the truth—or neglecting to obey God with a righteous life. And we certainly will have no protection if we are not saved in Jesus Christ. What about peace? How many times have you hung your head in sadness over someone who says they love the Lord but is gossiping and stirring up trouble instead of carrying a message of peace?

The devil knows our weakest spots. If we don't daily clothe ourselves completely in God's spiritual armor when we hit the rough bumps—sure enough —we come crashing down. That weak spot is bound to be injured and sometimes badly broken.

Like a parent with our roller-blade gear, God teaches us what to do for our own good, because He loves us.

So as you dress for your day and pray, remember to put on every single piece of God's armor. Then listen to Him.

Hear the Battle Cry

Comrades, hark to the call that is ringing
far and wide throughout the land!
O, hear it, answer the summons
that bids us to the fray.
See the host of the enemy, ranged on either hand,
Rank on rank, the fight is on today!
Now's the time when we must face the foe;
Now is the time when the loyal and true must
to the world their colors show.

Jesus, He is the one who will lead us in the fight we wage with sin.

He'll give us courage and strength for the time of sorest need.

Trusting all to the wisdom of Him we'll surely win,
Win the day, with Jesus Christ to lead.

Right shall win, and wrong shall meet with loss

If we but follow the Savior of men bearing the banner of the cross.

Comrades, rally from north and from south today, and come from east and west.

Christ needs you, answer the summons that calls us to the fight.

Gladly turn to the service that puts us to the test.

Brave and true, to dare, to dare and do for right.

Rally, rally, round the flag of white,

Earnest, and loyal, and true to the end, and we have put sin's host to flight.

Christ who leads is in the camp,
Listen, O my comrades, to the mighty tramp;
Tramp of the army that gathers today,
eager, earnest for the fray.
O 'tis a glorious sight,
That of legions on the way,
Ready to battle for right,
Hear the battle cry,
Behold the King draws nigh!

R.L.STUCKEY

GOD GOES BEFORE US

A gigantic fear looms over me with foreboding, cruel threats. The longer I cringe and shy away from it, the bigger the giant becomes. Before I know it, this monster towers completely over me and I feel helpless. I can't see over, under, around, or through it. It's just too big! But thank You, Lord God, You see the way through. I feel Your encouraging presence in my heart, and I know I'm not alone.

I have faced other giants. Each one seemed to attack me with crushing force. I have already learned the only way to get past them is to face each one straight on, in the name of You, my Lord Jesus Christ.

This time I utter a prayer of praise and thanksgiving for victories to come. I pick up Your sword, my Bible. I gather Your truths like five smooth stones: to think on You, to love, have hope, forgive, and be steadfast. With a hearty shout, I heave them at this devilish giant in the name of the Lord!

Sometimes the giants tumble instantly. Others crumble piece by piece. Either way, You are the victor and You never leave me.

Thank You for not requiring me to fight these giants by myself. Thank You for going before me.

FACING THE GIANTS

What are the giants in your life? How can God help you overcome them? I believe it is good not only to pray, but to turn to His Word for the answers. There are direction and power in prayer and God's Word.

Whatever these giants are in our lives, we must not run from them. We must face them head-on as David did with Goliath.

Put on your spiritual armor and stand firm, unafraid, trusting God for strength.

1. Truth. Put on the belt of truth. God is truth and no deception abides with His will.

2. Righteousness. Put on the breastplate of righteousness. As we repent of our sins, Jesus forgives us. Only through Him can we live a righteous life.

3. Peace. Put on the shoes of the gospel of peace. As we study God's Word and seek His will for our lives, He gives a peace beyond description. In turn, we can learn to carry that same peace to others.

4. Salvation. Put on the helmet of salvation. Know for sure with your heart and mind that you can count on God's salvation. All you must do is ask forgiveness for your sins and for Jesus to be Lord of your life. Then don't let the devil creep in with his subtle ways.

Resist the temptations, just like in the old song, "Oh, be careful, little eyes, what you see, ears what you hear, tongue what you say, hands what you do, feet where you go."

Deliberately, continually, turn your back on sin. God can help clear our thoughts and hearts and assure us of hope for the future.

5. Faith. Put on the shield of faith. Because He first loved us and called us to be His own, we can relax and trust in Him to fight our giants.

6. God's Word. Put on the sword of the spirit. God's Word—your Bible. Read it often. Carry it in your car, your briefcase, your purse, so you can slip it out from time to time and call on God for strength and direction. Keep it especially in your heart.

The exciting thing about all this is when we put on the full armor of God and obey Him, then we can stand back, call "TIMBERRR—" and watch the giants fall!

CHRISTIAN, DOST THOU SEE THEM?

Christian, dost thou see them, on the holy ground,
How the powers of darkness, rage thy steps around?
Christian! Up and smite them,
counting gain but loss,
Smite them by the merit of the holy cross!

Christian, dost thou feel them,
how they work within,
Striving, tempting, luring, goading into sin?
Christian! Never tremble! Never be downcast!
Gird thee for the battle, thou shalt win at last.

Christian, dost thou hear them,
how they speak thee fair?
"Always fast and vigil?
Always watch in prayer?"

Christian! Answer boldly,
"While I breathe I pray!"
Peace shall follow battle,
night shall end in day.

"Well I know thy trouble, O My servant true,
Thou art very weary—I was weary too;
But that toil shall make thee
someday all Mine own,
And the end of sorrow shall
be near My throne."
Amen

JOHN BACCHUS DYKES, 1868

THE TRUTH

In this complicated world, Lord, we are often tempted to seek the easiest or quickest way out of problems. Before we know it, others don't take us at our word, and we wonder why.

Thank You, dear Lord, for helping me gird myself with Your belt of truth so honor and trust will follow me wherever I go. I praise You for granting me strength so I can resist the slightest temptation to tell those little white lies.

In all these things I give You glory, honor, and praise.

Show me your ways, O LORD, teach me your paths; guide me in your truth and teach me, for you are God my Savior, and my hope is in you all day long.

PSALM 25:4–5 NIV

FALSE TEACHERS

A person I visited with seemed sensational and magnetic with a "supersized" appearance of love for You. For a short while I thought I would want to be like that.

You cautioned me, Lord. I turned to Your Word and listened to my pastor. I realized things did not line up. The individual didn't reflect the true things of God but reminded me of the wolf in sheep's clothing. Now I won't always believe what others say, even when they claim it is from You.

Thank You for making me watchful and giving me insight from Your wise leaders and Your Bible. I'm learning to test everything, to see if it is of You.

You are my Shepherd and I know Your voice, Lord. I will follow You. I will not waver, nor be tossed to and fro by capricious doctrines. I will praise You for Your guidance and faithfulness.

You, dear children, are from God and have overcome them, because the one who is in you is greater than the one who is in the world. They are from the world and therefore speak from the viewpoint of the world, and the world listens to them. We are from God, and whoever knows God listens to us; but whoever is not from God does not listen to us. This is how we recognize the Spirit of truth and the spirit of falsehood.

1 JOHN 4:4–6 NIV

Breastplate
of Righteousness

How can I be righteous, dear Lord, when I seem to mess up in one way or another every day? How can I begin to deserve Your love and approval? I feel so unworthy. I can't do this on my own. Yet I know You are always with me, ready to forgive and show me step by step how to obey and depend on You.

You have promised me in Your Word to provide me with Your breastplate of righteousness, when I have You first in my life. I ask again now, Lord, for You to arm me with it and fend off the fiery darts of temptation and trials the devil shoots at me.

Thank You for helping me daily to live as You want. How I praise You for giving me strength to lay aside all that isn't right in Your eyes. Through You I can count all else worthless as I focus on You, my God. You and I, Lord, are one.

Once my life was full of sin and darkness, but now You have forgiven me and set me free! Thank You that I don't have to worry about being good enough to be Your child. When I was wrong, I asked Your forgiveness and determined to live the way I should. You have already paid the price for me and have fulfilled God's laws and requirements in the Ten Commandments.

I pray for Your breastplate of righteousness to protect me from sin and harm. Through it may I reflect Your glorious light each day. Thank You for helping me. No more will I bow to worthless sin and destruction. Instead, I pray for You to let Your light shine through me onto others so they may also turn their hearts to You, my Lord Jesus Christ.

Search me, O God, and know my heart;
try me, and know my thoughts:
And see if there be any wicked way in me,
and lead me in the way everlasting.

Holy, holy, holy, is the LORD of hosts:
the whole earth is full of his glory.

Save us, O LORD our God, and gather us
from among the heathen,
to give thanks unto thy holy name,
and to triumph in thy praise.
Blessed be the LORD God of Israel
from everlasting to everlasting:
and let all the people say, Amen.
Praise ye the LORD.

PSALM 139:23–24, ISAIAH 6:3,
PSALM 106:47–48 KJV

RESISTING TEMPTATIONS

The temptations in this world attack me again and again. I can't overcome them on my own. But with You, Lord Jesus, it is possible. Thank You for how You have helped me hide Your Word in my heart. When I am tempted to do wrong, I can call on You for help and use the power of Your Scriptures for strength to do what is right.

Thank You for granting me wisdom and understanding. Thank You for helping me to resist even the most subtle temptation and choose Your ways. I long for my life to be good and my deeds to be accomplished wisely and with humility. Father, please don't let me allow any bitterness, envy, or self-ishness in my life. Let me not utter one boastful word. Remind me, I pray, not to look down on those less fortunate. These things are not of You.

In place of this, let me gain wisdom, motives that are pure, a peaceful spirit, a considerate, submissive attitude, boundless mercy, and a life producing Your nutritious, spiritual fruit. You help me and I praise You for a life of peace, joy, and righteousness!

Thank You for how You never lead me into temptation. You deliver me from such. I think how when You were tempted, each time You rebuked the devil with God's Word. Thank You for giving me that same power to resist temptation.

Lord, I know You called me to be a Christian. I know You want me to reflect You in all I say and do. Thank You for reminding me to live a holy life, pure and pleasing to You. I so easily get pulled into the "little sins" of this world. Thank You for each time You give me strength to run from even the slightest appearance of evil.

Right now, I nail my natural sinful nature to the cross. When faults, bad habits, or temptations creep in, I take them back to You where they are destroyed by Your power and might. Then with joy and thanksgiving, I bring glory to You, my God. There is no way I can resist these things in my own power.

I use Your Word, the sword of the Spirit, to fight against temptation. I call upon Your name each day for help, and I praise You for answering me.

I want to live a holy life for You. I give You my life, my all. As I sense Your cleansing presence, Lord Jesus, You and I are one.

Holiness and Humility

Someone asked a minister if he had ever received a second blessing since he was converted.

"What do you mean?" was the reply. "I have received ten thousand since the first."

A great many think because they have been holy once, they are going to be holy for all time after. But O, my friends. We are leaky vessels and have to be kept full. If we are going to be used by God, we must be very humble. Humility and holiness go together. A man that lives close to God will be the humblest of men. Let us keep near Him.

Dwight L. Moody

Spiritual Boldness

My knees tremble with fear when I know I must speak out for You, Lord. How thankful I am that Your presence surrounds me. You anoint me with a strength and power I don't have.

I say a quick prayer and open my mouth. A strange, loving authority overflows within me. My words are Your words. I marvel at how others stop, listen, and think about what I say. Thank You, too, for telling me when to close my mouth and let Your Holy Spirit take over.

How can You give such a marvelous thing as spiritual boldness? Somehow You help me get past the shyness. I know my help comes from You, Lord. Thank You for reminding me not to grow arrogant and take things into my own hands lest I be offensive and off-base with my words. I acknowledge Your teaching, urging me to be wise, gracious, and considerate as I speak.

I praise You, Lord, for using me to tell others the wonderful news of all the things You have done for me.

Let the words of my mouth, and the meditation of my heart, be acceptable in thy sight, O Lord, my strength, and my redeemer.

PSALM 19:14 KJV

CARRY GOOD CHEER

Carry good cheer to the lonely,
Weighted with burdens of earth;
Ever beguiling the weeping to smiling,
Go scatter the blessings of mirth.

Carry good cheer to the weary,
Those who may fall by the way;
Speak of salvation from sin and temptation,
To all who are learning to stray.

Carry good cheer in the morning;
Carry good cheer in the night.
Effort is sweeter and living completer,
If ever we walk in love's light.

G. B. WILLIAMS, 1916

ANITA CORRINE DONIHUE

BOLDNESS TO DO RIGHT

Boldness from God is:
To fear not when giving your all.
To shun not when risking for Christ.
To shrink not when standing for right.
To waver not in honesty and integrity.
To limit not the capacity to love.
To squelch not enthusiasm for Christ.
To seek not the limelight lest you fall.
To heed not those who speak wrong.
God's Holy Spirit helps us:
Be bold for the truth in His Spirit.
Be bold to serve Christ in His Spirit.
Be bold to tell of God's love in His Spirit.

In so doing, we shall be carried by the power of God over the deepest and most treacherous of life's challenges.

SHOES OF THE GOSPEL OF PEACE

Father, when discord and hurt feelings press in on me from all sides, I thank You for clothing me with the shoes of the gospel of peace.

Things could have gone much worse had I not listened to Your cautioning voice. My quick tongue might have spit out angry words of reproach that I would have never been able to take back. Instead, You gave me a calm spirit and a wise mind. Thank You, Lord, for being there with me.

I still faced the situation head-on, but You showed me how to do it in a spirit of truth and unconditional love.

When discipline or unwelcome answers are required from me, You help me speak in a healing, loving spirit. When hearts are aching, You help me empathize with encouraging words and deeds of kindness. I don't have answers to all life's problems, but I can carry the gospel, the good news of Your love and peace, what You have done for me, and all You can do for everyone who trusts You.

Thank You for teaching me to walk worthy of my calling as a follower of Christ, with strength, yet with humility, gentleness, and patience from Your Holy Spirit. I endeavor now to be up-front and truthful, avoiding gossip and deception, promoting unity in Your Spirit rather than division.

No matter what happens, I will not return evil for evil. Only You can avenge. Instead, I will overcome evil with good. The power to fight sin comes from You, Lord. I praise You for that!

Being clothed with the shoes of the gospel of peace is given to us through the indwelling of Your cleansing Holy Spirit. This armor surrounds me with a mindset which is pure, peace loving, kind, impartial, full of mercy. In learning to walk in this way, I will sow peace and harvest righteousness.

You have quickened my spirit once again, Lord. Thank You for keeping me alert and helping me watch and pray.

Repeatedly, I hear You come to me, warning, Don't stop praying.

Thank You for helping me cast all my cares on You, for watching over me. As I pray, You assure me of my salvation and how You have forgiven my sins. As I focus on You, Lord, You help me think clearly and assure me You have control over what lies ahead, not only for me but for my loved ones. Satan prowls about like a wild, hungry animal, seeking whom he can destroy. But when I pray, You stand before me, my Defender and Shield.

Thank You for Your guidance. Thank You for comfort when I'm tempted to worry. You are my dearest friend. You care about me with an understanding love. You listen to me pour out my concerns and joys. I treasure Your answers when they come.

While I watch and pray, the cares of life roll off my shoulders and I feel an indescribable peace—a peace that comes from You.

I lift my praise to You, Lord. My thoughts focus on You. You, my Lord, dwell within me and I in You.

Now, as I go about my duties, I will continue to pray. I don't say "amen" for good-bye, but "amen" for so be it. In You, my precious Lord, our conversation goes on day and night.

Do not be anxious about anything, but in everything, by prayer and petition, with thanksgiving, present your requests to God. And the peace of God, which transcends all understanding, will guard your hearts and your minds in Christ Jesus.

PHILIPPIANS 4:6–7 NIV

SHIELD OF FAITH

This struggle I'm going through frightens me, Lord. No one seems able to help. I feel so alone. I've tried and tried to solve problems on my own, but, alas, to no avail. The challenges are too great. I can't continue like this. Why have I waited so long to turn it all over to You? Please help me, Lord.

You have rescued me more times in the past than I can count. So I want to trust You again now during this trying time.

I can't just muster up faith in You with a snap of my fingers. Sometimes my faith is so weak I can barely express it to You. But You have promised if my faith is even as small as a grain of mustard seed, You will move these mountainous problems of mine or simply help me burrow through them. Either way, I know You are here and You will bless. Like that tiny granule of mustard seed, my faith can barely be detected. I am so thankful You recognize it, Lord.

Because I have taken a baby step in faith, Your Spirit goes before me with Your shield of faith. Thank You for it and the faith You give to me.

By Your strength and power, I can place all my trust in You rather than in puny human beings with all their weaknesses and sometimes poor choices.

I realize the battle we fight isn't against sinful people and circumstances. The battle is against evil spirits of the darkness that we can't see. They roam about this earth seeking to destroy all in their path.

By faith, You give me power over these evil spirits; they can't even reach me, for I am protected by the shield of faith of Your Holy Spirit.

Daily praises and thanksgiving are on my lips to You, dear Lord. I exalt You and give You glory for Your wondrous love and protection.

Do not be anxious about anything, but in everything, by prayer and petition, with thanksgiving, present your requests to God. And the peace of God, which transcends all understanding, will guard your hearts and your minds in Christ Jesus.

Finally, brothers, whatever is true, whatever is noble, whatever is right, whatever is pure, whatever is lovely, whatever is admirable—if anything is excellent or praiseworthy—think about such things.

Whatever you have learned or received or heard from me, or seen in me—put it into practice. And the God of peace will be with you.

PHILIPPIANS 4:6–9 NIV

FAITH TRIUMPHANT

May all of us have the faith in the Lord Jesus Christ which availeth, that faith which worketh by love, and so, though we have begun in the egg on earth, yet, through God's brooding, before we know it we shall chip the shell: and though we have lain so long coiled up and helpless, we shall begin to put forth plumes: and, disdaining the nest, and finding the ground chilly beneath our feet, with every gathering feather we shall pine for the air, and pining, begin to try those notes which we are yet to learn; and, at length, in some bright and beaded morning, we shall spread our wings, and rising above the tangle and the thicket, soar through the blue, singing to the gate of heaven.

HENRY WARD BEECHER

How Can We Praise in Faith—Believing?

When the odds seem impossible to overcome, we carefully, painfully seek God's will. But how do we go about actively praising Him in faith—believing? Is it an attitude? Words? Or does it go beyond that?

Faith soars above the mountains of uncertainty and utters a confidence and assurance in our Lord God. He has a precise way of tunneling through, going over or around, and finding the answers. Although we don't know what is around the next bend, we must give Him our unconditional trust.

Putting our faith in action and praising Him for answers to come means plugging up the hill and doing the best we can as we trust Him in the trek. Other times it is going ahead in faith—believing, knowing without a shadow of doubt what He has for us, even if it's outside our comfort zone! Either way, we must take time to rest our minds and emotions, becoming refreshed in His strengthening Holy Spirit.

The most difficult part for me in putting faith into action and praising Him for answers to come is when I must completely turn all over to God and take my hands off. I'm a doer, incredibly stubborn; I don't give up easily when I have a sense of direction from the Lord.

But what often comes is a time when I hear God say, "Hands off and let Me."

It is at this point where I learn to actively praise Him for helping, actively rest in His will and timing, actively trust Him to fight the battles as I learn to sit back and go along for the ride.

Faith in the negative comes from worry. Faith in the positive comes from unconditional trust in God.

FAITH THE ONLY DOOR

There is only one door into heaven; that door is faith. There is only one ship that sails for the skies: her name is Faith. There is only one weapon with which to contend with opposition; that is faith. Faith is the first step; faith is the second step; faith the third step; faith the fourth step; faith the last step. We enter the road by faith. We contend against adversaries by faith; we die by faith; heaven is the reward of faith.

T. DeWitt Talmage

Now faith is the substance of things hoped for, the evidence of things not seen.

Hebrews 11:1 KJV

IN YOU, I BELIEVE

I believe in You, Lord Jesus. Thank You for helping me not to be tossed to and fro on the gusts of fads, new gimmicks, propaganda. If not for You, I would be like a wandering sheep.

Thank You for helping me to seek and know Your truth. I praise You for giving me intelligence to search out right from wrong. Your Word is a lamp to

my feet and a light to my path. I praise You for leading. Through You, my life has become richer and
fuller with a deep, inner joy.

No matter what happens, no matter the influ-
ences, in You I will still believe and live.

Thank You for walking ahead of me, so I may
follow; for walking beside me, so I may know Your
fellowship; for staying close behind me, so I may be
protected. Each time I hear Your voice, I will follow.

In You, I believe. In You, I trust. In You, Lord
Jesus, are all of life's answers. You, my true God, are
sufficient! I need no other.

I know whom I have believed, and am persuaded that he
is able to keep that which I have committed unto him
against that day.

2 TIMOTHY 1:12 KJV

But as many as received him, to them gave he power to
become the sons of God, even to them that believe on his
name.

JOHN 1:12 KJV

I KNOW NOT WHY
GOD'S WONDROUS GRACE

I know not why God's wondrous grace
To me He hath made known,
Nor why, unworthy, Christ in love
Redeemed me for His own.

I know not how this saving faith,
To me He did impart,
Nor how believing in His word
Wrought peace within my heart.

I know not how the Spirit moves,
Convincing men of sin,
Revealing Jesus through the Word,
Creating faith in Him.

I know not when my Lord may come,
At night or noonday fair,
Nor if I'll walk the vale with Him,
Or meet Him in the air.

But "I know whom I have believed,
And am persuaded that he is able
To keep that which I've committed
Unto him against that day."

JAMES McGRANAHAN, 1883

My prayer of faith is being put to the test. Certainly, the trying of my faith works on my patience. Yet it requires much discipline from me and it is so frustrating!

I want everything done microwave-style, Lord—right now. I can't understand why my prayers aren't answered immediately. But even though I don't see the reasoning of it all, I still put complete confidence and faith in You, my God and King. I will trust in You with all my heart and I will lean not on my own understanding. I will continue turning to You and acknowledging Your Word so You may direct my paths.

Because of all You have done for me in the past, because of the promises in Your Word, my faith still holds fast to You, Jesus Christ, my Lord! I will put my faith into action and rest upon Your Word. I will praise You day and night for all Your mighty deeds.

My brethren, count it all joy when ye fall into divers temptations; Knowing this, that the trying of your faith worketh patience. But let patience have her perfect work, that ye may be perfect and entire, wanting nothing.

JAMES 1:2–4 KJV

FAITH IS THE VICTORY

Encamped along the hills of light,
Ye Christian soldiers, rise,
And press the battle ere the night
Shall veil the glowing skies.

Against the foe in vales below
Let all our strength be hurled.
Faith is the victory, we know,
That overcomes the world.

His banner over us is love,
Our sword the Word of God;
We tread the road the saints above
With shouts of triumph trod.

By faith they, like a whirlwind's breath,
Swept on o'er ev'ry field;
The faith by which they conquered Death
Is still our shining shield.

On ev'ry hand the foe we find
Drawn up in dread array.
Let tents of ease be left behind,
And onward to the fray.

Salvation's helmet on each head,
With truth all girt about,
The earth shall tremble 'neath our tread,
And echo with our shout.

To him that overcomes the foe
White raiment shall be giv'n;
Before the angels he shall know
His name confessed in heav'n.

Then onward from the hills of light,
Our hearts with love aflame;
We'll vanquish all the hosts of night
In Jesus' conqu'ring name.

Faith is the victory!
Faith is the victory!
O glorious victory
That overcomes the world!

IRA SANKEY

Thank You, God, for the helmet of salvation, for giving me full knowledge and assurance that You are my Savior and my Lord. When the devil tries to put doubts in my mind, that I am undeserving of Your love, that I am not really saved, Your promises planted sure and true in my brain tell me this is not true. Thank You, Lord, for shedding Your blood and saving someone as unworthy as me and making me Your beloved child.

Once I was a sinner, but thanks be to You, O God. You took the burden of all my sins into Your own Being and died on the cross. You paid the price for me so I can be free. Praise be to You. I am done with that old sinful life and have a new abundant one with You.

I can come before You with a clean heart because of what You have accomplished. You will live forever in me, and I in You. Each day, You assure me of how You removed my sins as far as the east is from the west. They are no more. No one, not even the devil himself, has the power to separate me from Your love. Since You loved me enough to save me, I can't imagine how many more blessings are in store as we go through this victorious life together!

Life may not always be easy. I may suffer for Your sake. But how much more You did for me in comparison. When I obey and do Your will, when I suffer, when I labor in prayer with You, sin loses its power. Then I see new victories in You, Christ Jesus, in the glory of Your name! So be it! Amen.

For the wages of sin is death, but the gift of God is eternal life in Christ Jesus our Lord.

ROMANS 6:23 NIV

YOUR SALVATION

Lord Jesus, You saw my sin but You forgave me in spite of it all. Thank You for drawing me close to You and comforting me in my lost state of sinfulness. I felt so distraught over my wrongdoings, I couldn't forgive myself. How could I expect You, the God of everything, to forgive someone like me? But You did.

You gently coaxed me. My knuckles turned white when I gripped the church bench in front of me during repeated altar calls. Thank You for assuring me that all my sins, no matter how dark the stains, could be removed and my life could become as fresh and clean as newly fallen snow. Though my sins were like crimson, You made me clean and white as a baby lamb's wool.

Thank You for granting me strength to come to You and for helping me fling the mess of my life at Your feet. As soon as I did, I felt a tremendous weight lifted from my shoulders. I was so happy, I had to tell everyone what You did for me.

I will bless You, my Lord, throughout my life. I will continually praise Your name. You turned me from sin, destruction, and hopelessness to a life of joyous freedom with You. Praise Your Name!

THE CROSS

Dear Jesus, I sit here in church and gaze at Your cross, praising You. Its story unfolds in my mind. The cross is lofty, beautiful before me, yet a symbol of pain and sacrifice. My heart saddens. I look upon it again and I see triumph, victory, a time of celebration.

I feel unworthy of all You did. I wince to think of Your beatings. Your crown of thorns, how nails pierced through Your hands and feet—pain few could endure. You bore the heavy cross to the place of the skull called Golgotha. How could Pilate have mocked You so by writing "Jesus of Nazareth, the King of the Jews" on that cross? Did he know in his heart the truth? That You were the King of all kings?

Tears fill my eyes at the thought of the mockery. I mourn the parting of Your garments, the gambling over them. The awful sins of the world weighed on Your shoulders, even while You saw to the care of Your mother and prayed to God to forgive all sin.

Then I hear Your agonizing words, "Eli, Eli, lama sabachthani? My God, my God, why hast thou forsaken Me?"

Did the Father really turn away, unable to look upon Your suffering, Lord Jesus, when You took our sins upon Yourself? I think of the way You refused the bitter vinegar to Your lips. You refused to call for angels to come and save You. Were they crying, too? Through Your pain, You still forgave the thief and welcomed him into paradise.

Your triumphant words penetrated all sin and darkness: "Father, into Thy hands I commend my spirit. It is finished."

What power Your Father released at that moment of exaltation! I cannot thank You enough for all You did, Lord. I offer my life of praise for Your dying on the cross and setting me free from sin. Thank You for rising again, thank You that the cross is now empty. I praise You, because of all You did, so I can have a victorious life in You.

THE CROSS IN THE CENTER

Look at the cross. Think of all the ways it is described to us. Composers have created marvelous songs. Painters and sculptors have tried to capture its meaning. Martyrs under persecution have clung to it. Christians find it a source of strength and healing in trying times.

The cross means more. It isn't only a lovely piece of art. It symbolizes all we believe in. It proclaims God's promise that we are set free from sin because Jesus died for us. It attests to the fact we really are saved by God's grace!

Think of the Lord Jesus who died on that cross. Take hold of His nail-pierced hands and don't let go. When darkness surrounds you and the earthquakes of life rumble like on the hill of Golgotha, know for sure that He has already provided the power to overcome anything and everything we face.

Call to remembrance the three crosses. Jesus hung on the center cross. He looked to one side and saw a thief who died an angry, unrepentant death. Jesus gazed at the man on the other side, another thief. This man begged for forgiveness and went on with Jesus to paradise.

See the cross in the center. The darkness is gone. Victory vibrates throughout the land. The veil in the temple has been split from top to bottom. No longer are we separated from the Holy of Holies! Death has been beaten. People are healed of sickness and pain. Those who have sinned are set free!

All the crosses mankind has manufactured will perish. But the victory and power that came from God's love for us and Christ dying on that cross in the center shall never perish. Storms of life cannot destroy it. Far-out doctrines cannot overshadow it. Evil rulers cannot crush it. Through any of these things and more, the power of God's love will break through.

In the cross of Christ I glory,
Towering o'er the wrecks of time;
All the light of sacred story
Gathers 'round its head sublime.

SIR JOHN BOWRING

ETERNAL LIFE

We must live our lives with eternity's values in full view. What of our high-tech military jets? Are they of any worth if they can't do battle when needed? All the planning and work we have done to serve God doesn't matter if we aren't willing to go into the battle for Christ and be faithful.

If the military planes fail to function properly, disaster occurs. Only in pressing forward for our God will we be able to see the victories (and the failures), but keep eternal life in full view.

We must continue marching and serving, refusing to break our stride with God. We must go right into eternity where He will still be with us. There is no end in death. A new, impelling power of God waits just beyond.

Greater than the tremendous force thrusting jets into the sky is God's power that launches us into a glorious life eternal with Jesus Christ, our Lord!

THE SWORD
OF THE SPIRIT

Thank You, Father, for the sword of the Spirit, Your Word, my Bible. Its truths and promises are precious to me. Its lessons are ageless. Your words are full of grace, wisdom, and power. I'm amazed at how so many lessons speak directly to my own life's situations, giving me direction on what to do.

Thank You for the authority in Your Word and for how I can claim its promises. It is a light to my pathway so I won't stumble. Your Word is all-powerful and cuts through to my heart's desires like a sharp two-edged sword and reveals that which is and is not pleasing to You. Teach me the right way, Lord.

Thank You for how Your Word breaks the devil's barriers and temptations. All I need to do is speak the words from Your Scriptures and he flees.

Your Word reveals Your mighty glory to those around me. Help me remember to use the verses I've learned to help others, but to say them wisely, with guidance from Your Holy Spirit.

Thank You for providing my Bible, the sword of the Spirit, to fight the spiritual battles.

Your word is a lamp to my feet
and a light for my path.
I have taken an oath and confirmed it,
that I will follow your righteous laws.

I have suffered much; renew my life,
O LORD, according to your word.
Accept, O LORD, the willing praise of my mouth,
and teach me your laws.

Though I constantly take my life in my hands,
I will not forget your law.
The wicked have set a snare for me,
but I have not strayed from your precepts.

Your statutes are my heritage forever;
they are the joy of my heart.
My heart is set on keeping your decrees
to the very end.

PSALM 119:105–112 NIV

ANITA CORRINE DONIHUE

Your Word

Praise be to You, O Father, for Your Word. Throughout eternity it shall always remain. I love to read and study it. My heart fills with peace as I meditate on it day and night.

Thank You for leading me through Your Word. It is a flashlight before my feet. Your Word, my Bible, provides a radiant beam and illuminates the exact, true way of the darkest pathways.

Oh, the secrets and marvelous mysteries of life You reveal to me! You lay out the answers as on a holy scroll. You teach me what I need in order to handle each situation. I see Your counsel and You grant me wisdom through Your Word. As I follow the advice in Your Scriptures, I find confidence and certainty in decisions to be made.

Thank You for providing my Bible. Its steadfast, true lessons will never change. I praise You that I can depend on them all my life. I will study and memorize their teachings so You can be pleased with me. I will trust You to help me understand as we go through my Bible together.

Study to shew thyself approved unto God, a workman that needeth not to be ashamed, rightly dividing the word of truth.

2 Timothy 2:15 KJV

I will obey your word.
Open my eyes that I may see
    wonderful things in your law.
I am a stranger on earth;
    do not hide your commands from me.
My soul is consumed with longing
    for your laws at all times.

Teach me, O LORD, to follow your decrees;
    then I will keep them to the end.
Give me understanding, and I will keep your law
    and obey it with all my heart.
Direct me in the path of your commands,
    for there I find delight.
Turn my head toward your statutes
    and not toward selfish gain.
Turn my eyes away from worthless things;
    renew my life according to your word.

May your unfailing love come to me, O LORD,
    your salvation according to your promise.

PSALM 119:17–20, 33–37, 41 NIV

THE BOOK THAT
NEVER GROWS OLD

There's a wonderful Book that appeals to my heart,
A mine of riches untold.
Ev'ry word is a jewel of luster divine,
The Book that never grows old.

Like a beacon of light doth it shine thro' the years,
To lead us safe to the fold.
Thro' the clouds that arise, gleaming brightly afar,
The Book that never grows old.

When billows of life would my bark overwhelm,
This anchor surely will hold.
Grounded deep in God's love are its promises sure,
The Book that never grows old.

It never grows old, no, never grows old,
The Word of the Father above.
It never grows old, no, never grows old.
Praise God for the Book of His love!

J. R. BAXTER, 1915

The Holy Spirit's power is as great today as ever. Through prayer and Bible reading, we have the same victories available to us as Jesus did when He was raised from the dead. But trite prayer isn't enough. Fasting, praying, and praising make the difference.

The late 1800s were as difficult times as now. Sin lurked everywhere. Lives and families were destroyed. One of the most powerful preachers of that day saw all this firsthand. Here is a little of his timeless wisdom.

Thomas Guthrie shared effectively when he described the greatness of the Holy Spirit's power. He challenged Christians that in hell's hottest fires the devil never forged a plan that God's Spirit, wielding the hammer of His Word, couldn't strike out.

Doctor Guthrie passionately encouraged Christians to put the Bible to the test. Along with it, he urged everyone to call on the power of prayer. He told how the Bible, coupled with sincere wrestling and laboring, breaks the chains of sin and darkness.

He went on to impel us to step into the inner prison where Peter was brought forth by the angel's hands. At this point we see the marvelous ways our prayers to God will be turned into victorious, grateful praises.

Blessed Be His Name

For unto us a child is born, unto us a son is given:
and the government shall be upon his shoulder:
and his name shall be called Wonderful, Counsellor,
The mighty God, The everlasting Father,
The Prince of Peace.

ISAIAH 9:6 KJV

Oh that men would praise the LORD for his goodness,
and for his wonderful works to the children of men!

PSALM 107:8 KJV

COUNSELOR, EVERLASTING FATHER

Thank You for being Counselor, Father. Through You I gain wisdom and direction. Your Word gives me good advice and common sense. Its Scriptures shed light on the paths before me and help me not to stumble.

I trust in You in all I do. I will keep Your will first place in all things. As I obey You, my Father, I thank You for blessing me with joy and success.

I don't have the foresight to chart the course for my life. You must be my Guide. Each day I sense You telling me, "Not that way. Go here, instead."

I entrust all I do to Your keeping, whether the way be difficult or easy.

I'm not able to understand why things happen, but I will leave the outcome in Your hands, my Father and Counselor. Then I will go on as You guide me with Your wisdom and direction. You are my God forever and ever. Praise be to You!

Thou shalt guide me with thy counsel, and afterward receive me to glory.

PSALM 73:24 KJV

YOUR COUNSEL

I toss and turn in my bed, trying to reach a right decision on how to deal with a difficult problem. Finally, after lying awake for hours, I arise and meet with You.

Thank You for Your counsel, Father. While I wait on You here in prayer, I feel Your help and guidance. I open Your Word and see more answers. Your Scriptures flow through my mind. I promise You to follow them. I'll copy them and place them as reminders in prominent places. I will hide them in my heart and draw on each one when I need them, so I can make wise choices.

You have given me the keys to solving my problems, Lord. Thank You for showing me the right way. Your counsel is so sensible and right. Your wisdom is sure and true. I return now to my bed and rest with peace of heart and mind.

There is no other so great as You, O Lord. You are my mighty God. Nowhere in heaven or earth is there One so wonderful and holy. I long to glorify Your mighty name every moment of each day. In all I do and say I give You honor and adoration.

Praise You for Your wonderful works, my God. So great are You who created heaven and earth and all the stars. So magnificent was Your plan to bring it all into being and put it into motion. You even stepped down here and saved a minute soul like mine.

You cause tides to change, mountains to grow. You start the heartbeat of a tiny, baby bird. You blow the breath of life into a newborn child.

Once You saw those you love go through wars. You plagued Pharaoh and the Egyptians. You parted the Red Sea, crushed rocks, and even softened hearts of stone.

How mighty You are, my God! How marvelous are the ways Your power works in each person who loves You. Great things happen beyond my dreams as I praise and trust Your mighty presence.

To You, O mighty God, be power and glory forever! Amen.

Among the gods there is none
  like unto thee, O LORD;
neither are there any works like
  unto thy works.
All nations whom thou hast made shall come and
worship before thee,
    O Lord; and shall glorify thy name.
For thou are great, and doest wondrous things:
    thou art God alone.

PSALM 86:8–10 KJV

YOUR MIGHTY WORKS

Sing out praises to the Lord,
All who dwell below.
Let heaven echo heartfelt words.
Let the anthems flow.
Sing the Creator's boundless work.
Tell of His wondrous love.
Praises, all praises from heart and soul,
Ascend to our God above.

Thank You, Lord Jesus, for being my Savior, my Prince of Peace. I praise You for breaking the power of sin and death and leading me into everlasting life. Through this, You have given me peace of heart and mind and a wonderful heritage in the family of God, our Father.

I can't comprehend how Your life-giving Spirit has made it possible for me to live forever. It is so wonderful. I need not fear the future, for my life is in Your hands. Thank You for the peace You give when life's uncertainties arise. I need not fear physical death, for I will be taken to be with You in glory. How awesome! How magnificent!

You are truly holy, Lord Jesus. You have been and are forever. You are my mighty God, my King above all rulers, my eternal Lord. I worship and praise Your name forever.

REDEEMER

Praise You, O Lord, for being my Savior, my Redeemer. Thank You for snatching me from a life of sin and hiding me safely in Your everlasting arms.

Because You live forever and You saw fit to love me, You have redeemed me and given me a wonderful life as Your child. I live because You live. I am free from sin because You set me free. Thank You for giving me joy indescribable and power to win a victorious life above the trials of this world. This gladness You give me each day would be out of my reach without my knowing You as my Redeemer.

Thank You for preparing a greater place for me and an unquenchable everlasting joy. The way to heaven would be impossible for me to find without You.

I lift my heart in praise to You, my Lord: my Way, my Truth, my Life, my Redeemer.

Let the words of my mouth, and the meditation of my heart, be acceptable in thy sight, O LORD, my strength, and my redeemer.

PSALM 19:14 KJV

KING OF KINGS

There are crowns worn by living monarchs, of which it would be difficult to estimate the value. The price paid for their jewels is the least part of it. They cost thousands of lives and rivers of human blood; yet in His esteem, and surely in ours also, Christ's crown outweighs them all. He gave His life for it; and alone, of all monarchs, He was crowned at His coronation by the hands of Death. Others cease to be kings when they die. By dying He became a king. He entered His kingdom through the gates of the grave, and ascended the universe by the steps of a cross.

THOMAS GUTHRIE

LORD OF LORDS

Lord, enthroned in heavenly splendor,
First begotten from the dead.
Thou alone, our strong defender,
Liftest up Thy peoples' head.

Here our humblest homage pay we;
Here in loving reverence bow;
Here for faith's discernment pray we
Lest we fail to know Thee now.

Alleluia! Alleluia! Alleluia!

GEORGE HUGH BOURNE, 1874

ELOHIM, STRONG CREATOR, LORD OF ALL CREATION

How I rejoice in You, O Lord, for You are right and good. I try to come to You with a pure heart so You may be pleased with my praise offering. I create a new song to You, for You are holy.

Thank You for all You have created. You are Lord of everything. All You have made has been done with goodness and righteousness. The earth is filled with Your virtue. You breathed and the heavens rolled into place. You scooped up the waters and furrowed out deep storage places for them. When You spoke, the whole world trembled. At Your command, all was complete and stood firm. Let all You have created stand and gaze at You in awe.

How puny are the plans of great leaders, their efforts to control this earth and all therein, in comparison with Your mighty works. Your wisdom sees beyond all generations. You know our needs on this earth and have everything under Your omnipotent control.

You reach down from heaven. Miraculously, You mold and direct each willing heart. You lead those who trust in You to make wise choices in caring for the earth You have entrusted to our care.

Safety from earthquakes, famine, and storms will not come from clever scientific designs, but from You, the One who created it all.

Those who love You wait on You, O Lord. You are our protection, our help, our strength, our shield, our Creator. We rejoice in You and place our trust in Your holy name.

Thank You for our beautiful world. When we make unwise choices, we thank You for Your patience and mercy. Help us always to be wise through Your counsel. May we place our hope and trust in You, the Creator of it all.

And God saw every thing that he had made, and, behold, it was very good.

GENESIS 1:31 KJV

Rejoice in the Lord, O ye righteous:
>   for praise is comely for the upright.
Praise the Lord with harp:
>   sing unto him with the psaltery
>   and an instrument of ten strings.
Sing unto him a new song;
>   play skilfully with a loud noise.
For the word of the Lord is right;
>   and all his works are done in truth.
He loveth righteousness and judgment:
>   the earth is full of the goodness of the Lord.
By the word of the Lord were the heavens made; and all the host of them by the breath of his mouth.
He gathereth the waters of the sea together as an heap:
>   he layeth up the depth in storehouses.
Let all the earth fear the Lord:
>   let all the inhabitants of the world
>   stand in awe of him.
For he spake, and it was done;
>   he commanded, and it stood fast.

PSALM 33:1–9 KJV

My Emmanuel, how grateful I am for You being with us through the generations of mankind. You were there with Adam and Eve. How wonderful it must have been to be able to walk and talk with You. No sin. No strife.

Even after Adam and Eve sinned, You still made a way of communing with Your people. You had more planned for us, and I praise You for it. You brought forth the gift of Your only Son onto this earth so we could be with You again. Thank You for how Jesus became human and lived with us, showing right from wrong. Your kindness, holiness, and love were a living example.

I can't imagine how frightened the followers of Jesus were when He died. They thought they were losing their beloved Master. You showed again Your tremendous power when Jesus stepped through locked doors to be with His grieving disciples and friends. They must have been shocked and thrilled at the same time. Thomas couldn't believe his eyes. What our Savior did with Thomas at that moment has increased the faith of many after all these years. Thank You for how He showed Thomas His hands, His feet, His side, and how our Lord Jesus told him to have faith and believe. Finally, Thomas did trust in the Son of God standing before him.

I praise You, Emmanuel, for being with me now. You sent Your Holy Spirit to help and comfort me. Thank You for walking and talking with me, for guiding me each day. I sense Your presence and know

Your voice. I'm so glad You are here, my dear Emmanuel. Blessed be Your name.

And surely I will be with you always, to the very end of the age.

MATTHEW 28:20 NIV

TAKE COMFORT

Do you ever feel your trials are like wearing a crown of thorns? Be faithful. As you trust in God, your crown of thorns will be taken away and He will hand you a crown with stars instead. Remember to thank and praise Him.

Do you feel like you are overloaded, your hands filled with heavy cares? Be faithful. As you keep trusting in God, He will take away your heavy cares and place a harp in your grasp, so you may sing glory and honor to God for all He has done. Remember to thank and praise Him.

Do your garments feel soiled with dirt and grime from struggling in a sin-sick world? Stay faithful. He will replace them with clothing that is shining white. Remember to thank and praise Him.

Hold on and do not despair. There will be a time when you look back and your trials will seem as nothing in light of the many answered prayers, miracles, and evidence of God's glory and grace.

When we meet in heaven, our adversities will become strangely dim in the shadows of God's unfailing love. Remember to thank and praise Him.

Step by step, day by day, He takes each trial and turns it inside out. Triumphs emerge like a marvelous spiritual metamorphosis. Each of your obedient acts will be transformed to joy unspeakable!

So, take heart. Stay faithful. When all is ever so dark, know for sure morning follows the night.

When the dawn breaks through, remember to lift your heart in thanksgiving and praise to the One who gives all comfort and help.

COMFORTER

When Jesus bid His friends farewell,
He promised peace would remain.
The Holy Spirit came to earth,
The Comforter in His name.

CHURCH

For Your church, my heavenly Father, I thank You. Thank You for founding it, for purchasing it with the blood of Your Son, Jesus Christ. Not a building, but a courageous body of believers who through the years have given their all to be able to worship You. Your church has persevered, enduring wars, tribulations, bountiful blessings, and heartbreaking failures.

For the love of Jesus that has bound Your church body together through the ages, I praise You. For those who bravely stepped forward, accepted Him as their Savior, were cleansed, baptized, and went on to give a lifetime of service to You, I thank You.

Although riddled with arrows from the evil one, Your church stands. When razor-sharp tongues attempt to amputate parts of its precious body, it still remains and comes back stronger than ever as we trust in and obey You.

As I watch on our day of worship, I see many people who mean so much: the custodians; those who bring flowers; others involved with refreshments; the organizers, donators, youth, and children; the parents, elders, music groups, pastors, pastors' wives; the missionaries; and (bless their hearts) the prayer warriors. The list goes on and on. When one isn't in church, there's a gap. No one in Your family is less or more important than any other. Each one matters to You, and I thank You for them.

Thank You for asking me to be part of Your church. I praise You for giving us the ability to love and give to one another. When one is happy, we all rejoice. When another is hurting, we hurt with them, pray for and help them. Little by little, we are learning to become soul winners. Thank You for helping us to constantly reach out and invite new people into Your family.

In light of Your presence, I am grateful for these, my dear family of God, who care about and love me. The bond we share may or may not be biological. It is one that is sealed by the blood of Your Son, Jesus Christ. Thank You for how You provide the same power that raised Jesus from the dead and gave us eternal life to protect, care for, and increase this holy church throughout the ages.

Let the filling of Your cleansing Holy Spirit within this church begin within my heart. May all we say and do please and glorify You. Praise be to You, my heavenly Father, for Your church.

God's Church Is Alive and Well

Some people feel the church is dying. Praise God, throughout the entire world His church is alive and well! She may be trampled, threatened, burned, blown up, misunderstood, mistreated, and ignored, yet her heartbeat grows stronger. The saints march forward and speak out for Christ more and more every day.

Although they are important, the church is not just things like choirs, organs, sermons, and social activities. She is made up of servants of God, with Jesus Christ as her foundation. Every believer is part of the Body of Christ.

The church will never die. It is eternal. We, as part of the church, must step forth and share the good news of what God has done for us with everyone and anyone who will listen. There is an urgency in this, for life here on earth is short. This is our commandment: to tell the world about the love of Jesus.

When you feel reserved or frightened about testifying of Jesus, think how you would feel if you inherited a million dollars. Could you keep quiet? Or would you shout for joy and tell all your friends the good news?

Christ paid our debt of sin and gave all who accept Him the most valuable gift of all: an abundant, joyful life on earth and eternal life with God in heaven. And it didn't cost us a thing except submitting to His will and accepting His gift. Most incredible is that we can share this wonderful gift with those around us, so they may also receive Him. Our friends, our family, the hairdresser, the store clerk, our coworkers, the gas station attendant—the list goes on and on.

Stand up for Jesus. Use the Word of God for your guide. Help lead others to Christ. If you need assistance, call on a Christian friend or your pastor to help. But, you can also pray with someone all by yourself. What a thrill it is to watch a baby soul be born in the Lord!

Rejoice as the heart of the church beats stronger and stronger, and the glory of the Lord overshadows all else.

Consequently, you are no longer foreigners and aliens, but fellow citizens with God's people and members of God's household, built on the foundation of the apostles and prophets, with Christ Jesus himself as the chief cornerstone.

In him the whole building is joined together and rises to become a holy temple in the Lord. And in him you too are being built together to become a dwelling in which God lives by his Spirit.

EPHESIANS 2:19–22 NIV

Your Altar

Here I stand in Your sanctuary, Lord Jesus, hungry, thirsty for Your closeness. The last hymn is being sung. I want to throw myself on Your altar, but what will people think? Will they view me as a troubled, lost soul or might they grant me those few moments of peace at Your footstool? No one else is up there. Will I disrupt things?

Lord, Your altar is precious to me. I know You are nudging me right now to simply kneel there for a moment, to drink from Your living water and share my thoughts with You. I can't let my pride come before You.

I push one foot forward. As quietly as possible, I slip to one end of Your altar and feel Your overwhelming love and strength. What is that vibration in the floor I feel? Why, here come another and another to pray.

Thank You for Your nudging Spirit, dear Lord. Thank You for meeting me here, again.

GOD'S FOOTSTOOL

The week had been exceptionally long. I was tired and had a lot on my mind. Yet, as a pastor's wife, I felt I must always be "the strong one."

Our church altar is always open to those who wish to go forward and pray or ask others to pray with them. But the pastor's wife? What would people think?

I longed to have that refreshing, strengthening moment at the altar. I like to think of it as God's footstool.

I brushed away the pride and stepped quietly forward. I knelt at one end, trying to seem invisible. But the very moment my knees hit the altar, a sense of His glorious Holy Spirit flooded over me. I could feel His power and strength rejuvenate me. His presence surrounded me like a warm, soft, lingering blanket.

I've learned to go frequently to God's footstool, not just for my needs, but for the needs of other dear ones to be lifted up in prayer.

I'm thankful God helped me shed my pride and take that first step.

Father, I'm grateful to You for giving me my church family. I stand back and watch as they bustle about, always looking for ways to encourage one another. I can never keep up with the blessings I receive from my church family, the family of God.

When advice is needed, they are quick to listen and slow to offer opinions. When advice is given, it is fruitful, like shiny apples in a finely woven basket.

Brothers and sisters in Christ often share and encourage each other in God's love. Tiny clusters of believers form, holding up needs in prayer. Cards and letters with encouraging words heal the downtrodden. True, growing believers never put one another down. Thank You for the example they set for our young people and new Christians. Thank You for caution shown in lives so no one is caused to stumble. Thank You for older people "adopting" younger couples, for the younger watching out for the elderly. For prayers and praises given for each other, I am so thankful. Bless these helpers and prayer warriors, dear Lord.

Thank You for my priceless church family.

And let us consider how we may spur one another on toward love and good deeds. Let us not give up meeting together, as some are in the habit of doing, but let us encourage one another.

HEBREWS 10:24–25 NIV

The upcoming move across the country was unexpected. James received a memo at work that he would be transferred from Seattle to Texas.

His wife, Danielle, and their two sons received the news that night with mixed emotions. They had roots in Seattle. Both sets of parents lived nearby, and James, Danielle, and the boys didn't want to leave them. The family members worshiped together and were active in their nearby church. The boys loved their church youth group.

The time came for them to move. Tears and hugs mingled as they climbed into the family car and followed the moving van.

When they arrived at the Texas house the company had waiting, it seemed strange. How long would it take to feel like home?

The first Sunday, James and Danielle took the boys to a nearby church they had located earlier in the week. The reception was cold, uncaring. They felt discouraged. Would they find a church family as loving as the one back home?

The following Sunday the family visited another church and was enthusiastically welcomed. The sermon met the family's needs. A potluck followed. James, Danielle, and the boys were able to get acquainted.

Danielle missed her mother more than anyone. She prayed for God to give her a Christian friend who could be like a second, away-from-home mom.

The next day the doorbell rang. A middle-aged woman with a big smile stood on the porch holding a casserole dish. She introduced herself as Ardella

Murphey, who lived two doors down and had seen James and Danielle at church the day before. Danielle invited her in. The two became friends. Danielle learned Ardella's husband had recently passed away and she was very lonely. James found a new friend in his same line of work. The boys settled in nicely with their new church youth group.

Weeks went by. Danielle and Ardella grew so close that Ardella became the substitute mom Danielle needed. James, Danielle, and the boys gave thanks and soon settled in with their second family, their church family of God.

FAITHFULNESS

How wonderful to know You continually keep me in mind, dear Lord. I can't comprehend how You watch over me day and night. When I rest my head on the pillow, You are there. When I rise in the morning, I can greet You and thank You for a new day. I praise You for how Your sweet presence surrounds me.

As I read my Bible and commune with You, I am nourished by Your Word. You surround me with Your presence like the fragrance of roses in full bloom.

How I praise You for loving me with an unwavering love. It surpasses all else. Your presence goes beyond all limits. It is stronger and more powerful than any mountain.

As You walk me through my day, You unfold Your lessons so I might listen and not err. I'm learning to heed Your guidance rather than react unwisely to whatever comes my way.

Thank You for letting me take refuge within Your protecting wings. Thank You for supplying my needs, feeding me physically and spiritually, allowing me to drink from Your living water.

My heart is full of Your exquisite joy as You honor me with Your constant presence. You are so wonderful, my God! To You I give glory, honor, and praise.

Providing for My Needs

How thankful I am, Lord, that I don't have to depend only on my own resources to provide for my needs. My happiness isn't dependent upon earthly treasures. Instead, You know very well what I need.

When I do the best I can to make ends meet, I remember I belong to You and You will help me. As I trust in You and share my tithes with You, I will not lack in what You know I need. Thank You for not withholding the good things from me as I follow along Your paths of righteousness. I trust in You.

When I'm tempted to toss and turn because of financial worries, I can cast my cares upon You and thank You already for answers to come. Then as I trust in You, I have a peace greater than anyone can comprehend.

Have You counted the hairs on my head? (I must keep You busy when I tear my hair out from worry. Forgive my distrust, Lord.) Do You really know each time a sparrow falls? How valued am I? Certainly more than a bird, yet they are important, too.

Each time I work to make the money stretch, remind me, Lord, to come to You with even the small needs. I know You care about those, too. I praise You for each blessing and miracle You give.

I will bless the LORD at all times:
    his praise shall continually be in my mouth.
My soul shall make her boast in the LORD:
    the humble shall hear thereof, and be glad.
O magnify the LORD with me,
    and let us exalt his name together.
I sought the LORD, and he heard me,
    and delivered me from all my fears.

This poor man cried, and the LORD heard him,
    and saved him out of all his troubles.
The angel of the LORD encampeth round about
    them that fear him, and delivereth them.
O taste and see that the LORD is good:
    blessed is the man that trusteth in him.

The young lions do lack, and suffer hunger:
    but they that seek the LORD
        shall not want any good thing.

The eyes of the LORD are upon the righteous,
    and his ears are open unto their cry.

The righteous cry, and the LORD heareth,
    and delivereth them out of all their troubles.
The LORD is nigh unto them that are of
    a broken heart; and saveth such as be
        of a contrite spirit.

PSALM 34:1–4, 6–8, 10, 15, 17–18 KJV

PRAISE YOU,
BECAUSE OF . . .

To whom or what could I compare You, O Lord? Can any begin to measure the waters with the palm of a hand as You can? Is there one who is able to know the breadth and height of the heavens or earth's contents? Where is one who can weigh and balance the mountains, the foothills? There is no one.

Who knows all the movements of God's Spirit other than You? Can any see what all Your plans are for our future? Does one person know the day of Your return? There is no one.

The earth, these tiny nations, are less than a drop in a bucket or a speck of dust in Your immense vision. So with all this, how are You mindful of me? How do You know me by name? My joys? My heart-cries? How is it that You love me?

I cannot fathom it, Father. I only know You are my everlasting God. You never grow faint or weary in caring for me. Your strength goes beyond all other means I depend upon. Even with all our technology, You are even greater. You control the balance of it all. Because of this, why should I fear?

Thank You for how You give me strength as I wait upon You. You teach me to mount up on Your wings as a baby eagle. Through Your strength, I can run and not be weary, I can walk and not faint.

This is why I praise You, Father.

HALLELUJAH, PRAISE JEHOVAH!

Hallelujah, praise Jehovah!
From the heavens praise His name.
Praise Jehovah in the highest;
All His angels, praise proclaim.

All His hosts, together praise Him—
Sun, and moon, and stars on high.
Praise Him, O ye heav'n of heavens,
And ye floods above the sky.

Let them praises give Jehovah;
They were made at His command.
Them forever He established;
His decree shall ever stand.

From the earth, oh, praise Jehovah,
All ye floods, ye dragons all;
Fire, and hail, and snow, and vapors,
Stormy winds that hear Him call.

All ye fruitful trees and cedars,
All ye hills and mountains high,
Creeping things and beasts and cattle,
Birds that in the heavens fly.

Kings of earth and all ye people,
Princes great, earth's judges all;
Praise His name, young men and maidens,
Aged men, and children small.

Let them praises give Jehovah,
For His name alone is high,
And His glory is exalted,
Far above the earth and sky.

WILLIAM J. KIRKPATRICK,
LATE 1800S

ALL YOU HAVE DONE

You have led me through so many wildernesses in my life, Father. Sometimes I even needed forty years, like Moses, to find my way out. Oh, the testing and trials along the way. The darkness, the storms, the frightening shadows, and the fears for the future. At times I couldn't see my way. Would the sun ever shine again? The struggles reduced my spirit to humiliation, defeat, and nothingness. I couldn't see the point of it all, only the agony. But You could.

When I had nowhere to go, I finally started to obey You, my heavenly Father. Thank You for walking by and finding me along the wilderness path. Your directions were right, Your lessons, true. Even the trials taught me wisdom and made me strong.

Once, when things were easy, I had become careless. But the trials caused me to cling to You, Father.

I don't know how I made it through each wilderness, except for all You did to help me. Somehow the miracles of time and circumstance fell into place.

You are a dear Father to me, understanding and caring. You took a little person like me, struggling along the wilderness way. You tended, fed, and watered me until I came into full bloom for Your glory. Then You brought me out to the other side where the sun shone brightly again. Thank You for all You have done.

A Rare Jewel

I proudly gazed at sixteen-year-old Michelle as she once again helped a group of our Church School children memorize Bible verses. Her long blond hair fell softly forward when she bent close with a listening ear. A shy little girl with clasped hands behind her back whispered her newly learned verse. Afterward, Michelle praised her for a job well done.

The first time I met Michelle was when she started coming to our church about two years ago. I thought at the time she had something special about her. I almost could see "leadership" printed right across her forehead.

It wasn't long until Michelle accepted my invitation to help me in Bible Explorer's Club. The program is built on individualized Bible memorization, so I'm always grateful for assistance.

I was delighted to discover that Michelle had studied the same program as a child. She jumped right in like it was second nature.

Last Christmas Michelle accepted the job of directing our children's Christmas program. She rewrote the script, recruited faithful helpers, and produced a successful program for us all to enjoy.

Michelle has many wonderful abilities far beyond her years. But the one that shines above them all is her commitment to faithfulness. We have all seen people who possess the abilities—but if you can't depend upon them, none of that matters. Keeping a promise is important to Michelle, a marvelous attribute for a teenage girl.

She is a rare jewel. I love her and appreciate her. I wish I could keep her forever. Thank you, Michelle, for your faithfulness.

HELPING ME TO BE FAITHFUL

My delight is in You, my Lord! I refuse to follow the footsteps of those who will not listen to You. If they should scorn Your ways, I will defend You with all my might.

Day and night I fix my thoughts on Your wise Word and praise You for it. My roots sink deeply in Your teachings so I may drink from Your living water. When the fiery trials and temptations come, I shall not wither. I will stand firm on Your promises, O Lord. No matter what happens, I will keep on producing Your spiritual fruit.

How I praise You. Each time I obey You, whatever I do prospers and the glory goes to You, Lord.

I grieve for the ungodly who refuse to turn their hearts to You. Their lives are headed for destruction. When they do evil, they won't prosper in the long run. They will become like chaff in the wind. How sad for them to not be able to lift their faces to You, unless they open their hearts. Should they stand in the presence of the believer, they will be overwhelmed with Your presence. Please, I pray You to help them turn to You, rather than flee from Your loving call. Even though these people's actions pierce my heart, I still hold them up to You in prayer so they, too, can know You as their Savior.

How righteous You are, O Lord! How awesome that You know my thoughts and ways. You know my going out and my coming in. You know my victories and rejoice with me. You are aware of my failures, yet You forgive me. When I am weak, You give me strength to be faithful to You. Thank You, dear Lord, for seeing my joys and smiling with me. I praise You for hearing my heart-cries and comforting me.

You are my Savior, my Friend, my Delight, my Song. By Your strength, I shall always be faithful. Blessed be Your name, my Lord!

$\mathcal{F}$ORGIVENESS

Father, before I gave my heart to You, my life had no direction or meaning. I was going nowhere fast. Then You spoke to me. You kept urging me to give my all to You. I could not. I wanted control. Where did that get me? Into more heartache and trouble.

I often stood in a church service hearing salvation's call. While we stood singing "Just As I Am," I clenched my teeth and squeezed the church bench in front of me until my knuckles turned white.

The time and season came when You softened my heart and tenderly called me to Your throne of grace. I finally asked You to forgive my sins. I placed everything in Your hands. My sins, so many, took flight. A huge load lifted from my shoulders. Your Son, Jesus Christ, paid the price over two thousand years ago so I could be set free. You forgave me, then cleansed and healed my wayward heart.

How wonderful and marvelous You are! Although I have sinned and come short of Your glory, You sent Your Son not to condemn, but to save even me. You gave Your gift of an abundant, joy-filled, eternal life. Thank You, heavenly Father.

You are the Way, the Truth, the Life. I came to You through Your Son, Jesus Christ, and You adopted me as Your own.

Once I was lost. Now I am found. I was blind. Now I see. I give thanks to You, for You are God. I exalt Your holy name.

For God so loved the world, that he gave his only begotten Son, that whosoever believeth in him should not perish, but have everlasting life. For God sent not his Son into the world to condemn the world; but that the world through him might be saved.

JOHN 3:16–17 KJV

Bless the LORD, O my soul:
    and all that is within me,
        bless his holy name.
Bless the LORD, O my soul,
    and forget not all his benefits:
Who forgiveth all thine iniquities;
    who healeth all thy diseases;
Who redeemeth thy life from destruction;
    who crowneth thee with lovingkindness
        and tender mercies;
Who satisfieth thy mouth with good things;
    so that thy youth is renewed like the eagle's.
The LORD executeth righteousness and judgment
        for all that are oppressed.

The LORD is merciful and gracious,
    slow to anger, and plenteous in mercy.
He will not always chide:
    neither will he keep his anger for ever.
He hath not dealt with us after our sins;
    nor rewarded us according to our iniquities.
For as the heaven is high above the earth,
    so great is his mercy toward them that fear him.
As far as the east is from the west,
    so far hath he removed our transgressions from us.

PSALM 103:1–6, 8–12 KJV

In the midst of the darkness and gloom of the cross, there came a voice from one of those thieves. It flashed into the soul of Jesus as He hung there, "This must be more than man; this must be the true Messiah." He cried out, "Lord, remember me when Thou comest into Thy Kingdom!"

We are anxious to get the last word of our dying friends. Here was the last act of Jesus. He snatched the thief from the jaws of death by saying, "This day shalt thou be with me in Paradise."

Such was His forgiveness of sin, an act of grace, just as His forgiveness of His murderers was an act of mercy.

DWIGHT L. MOODY

Thank You for
Taking Me Back

Father, I was just like that younger son who packed his bags, took his inheritance, and left his father, choosing a life of sin in a faraway land. After loving and serving You, I also chose to go astray and dabble in the sins of this world.

Thank You for freely taking me back with open arms when I came running to You with a repentant heart. Thank You for all You have done for me and for Your wonderful, forgiving love. Your mercy is so rich. You gave me life again. How I praise You!

Thank You for forgiving me—again. I cannot comprehend how You never hold a grudge against me. Instead, I know my sins are completely washed away. Your love is far greater than how high the heavens are above this little round ball called Earth. Your love stretched farther than the east is from the west. Thank You for being my tender, understanding Father.

I praise You over and over, Lord. Once I was lost. Now I am found and rejoice as a part of the family of God. I can finally see what real love is in You, Christ Jesus, my Savior. Thank You for welcoming me home.

FORGIVENESS

When on the fragrant sandal tree,
The woodman's ax descends,
And she who bloomed so beauteously
Beneath the keen stroke bends,
E'en on the edge that brought her death,
Dying, she breathes her sweetest breath,
As if to token in the fall
"Peace to my foes, and love to all!"
How hardly man this lesson learns,
To smile, and bless the hand that spurns;
To see that blow, and feel the pain,
But render only love again!
This spirit ne'er was given on earth;
One had it—He of heavenly birth;
Reviled, rejected, and betrayed,
No curse He breathed, no plaint He made,
But when in death's deep pang He sighed,
Prayed for his murderers and died.

AUTHOR UNKNOWN, LATE 1800s

And forgive us our debts, as we forgive our debtors.

MATTHEW 6:12 KJV

ANITA CORRINE DONIHUE

Lord, thank You for helping me praise You in my most broken and angry moments. How can I forgive, Lord, when I am cut down and mistreated repeatedly? I know You say seventy times seven, but I don't have it in my heart to do so. I again call upon You for help. Although I don't want to forgive, Lord, I ask You to change my heart.

Little by little, I feel You peel away the layers of bitterness. Like a big smelly onion, my angry spirit is a sting and irritant to the souls around me and even to myself. This must hurt You, too, Lord, to see me like this. I'm beginning to realize my unforgiveness separates me from You, Lord.

How can I get over the pain and frustration? It has grown and festered into a huge spiritual and emotional boil. It eats away at me to the point that I feel physically ill. I don't want to be like this, Lord. Although the process of Your working in me is as painful as lancing an infected boil, I pray for You to cleanse, forgive, and heal me.

Thank You for helping me to back off so I can look at all these hurts with a better perspective. Evil has been manipulating not only my offenders, but me, too. Thank You for giving me the insight to pray for those who spitefully use me. Please help them to accept You as their Savior. I pray for them to be set free from wrongdoing so they, too, may experience Your joy-filled abundant life.

Thank You for showing me how to love them with a love that comes from You, even when all is not right. I realize now I don't have to agree with them in order to forgive. I don't have to set myself up for them to continue to hurt me, nor do I need to unwisely trust them. But I must forgive, even if they aren't sorry or haven't changed.

Thank You for teaching me to let go and turn it all over to You. Your wisdom will work in their lives.

Thank You for helping me see where I have erred. You are teaching me to admit where I'm wrong, and if needed, to ask forgiveness. What if my apology is not accepted? Then I leave it in Your hands, Lord.

You have showed me the answer is not whether all is resolved. The answer is for You to create a pure, clean heart in me. I must do right in Your eyes and leave the rest in Your hands. I must forgive as You have forgiven me. After all this, I trust and praise You for Your wisdom and love.

If hurts return, I again take them to You and lay them at Your feet. You are my Healer, Redeemer, Counselor, Defender, and my Source of peace and strength. Thank You, Lord. Praise be to You!

Forbearing one another, and forgiving one another. . . even as Christ forgave you, so also do ye.

Colossians 3:13 kjv

RIENDSHIP

GOD TREASURES ME

Father, I praise You for treasuring me. Thank You for being my dearest Friend and reminding me:

- When I felt worthless,
  You developed my abilities.

- When I felt I lacked beauty,
  You reminded me of the
      inner beauty You gave me.

- When I was unworthy,
  You showed me Your love and instilled worth in me.

- When I wept over my sins,
  You forgave me.

- When I tried and failed,
  You bridged the gap.

- When I felt I had nothing to offer,
    You saw potential in me.
- When others didn't seem to care,
    You adopted me as Your child,
        and You treasured me as Your own.

O LORD, thou hast searched me,
    and known me.
Thou knowest my downsitting and mine uprising,
    thou understandest my thought afar off.
Thou compassest my path and my lying down,
    and art acquainted with all my ways.
For there is not a word in my tongue,
    but, lo, O LORD, thou knowest it altogether.
Thou hast beset me behind and before,
    and laid thine hand upon me.

I will praise thee; for I am fearfully
    and wonderfully made: marvellous are thy works.

Search me, O God, and know my heart:
    try me, and know my thoughts:
And see if there be any wicked way in me,
    and lead me in the way everlasting.

PSALM 139:1-5, 14, 23-24 KJV

Your Voice

I hear You speaking to my heart again, Lord. I know Your voice, for I have heard it so many times before. Without hesitation, I stop and listen, ready to experience Your fellowship, love, and direction.

You speak to me as I sleep at night, You calm and direct me through each busy day. I love Your voice and I praise You for speaking to my heart.

When You say, "Go," I go. When You say, "Come to Me," I follow.

I listen carefully to all You say. You speak peace to my soul. How wonderful and wise are Your words! Thank You, Lord Jesus, for Your voice.

I will hear what God the LORD will speak: for he will speak peace unto his people, and to his saints.

PSALM 85:8 KJV

God's Voice

How wonderful it is when God speaks to our hearts. He warns us of entrapments and consoles us in sadness. How satisfying to feel the warmth of His approval when we've done right.

Sometimes we get so busy we unknowingly tune God out, just like flipping the switch on the car radio. He wants us to stay in tune. Each time we listen carefully for His still small voice throughout the day, we experience joy and peace. Then we are thankful we listened. He helps us avoid a lot of mistakes and heartaches.

When we pray, we are tempted to whisper a quick prayer, jump up, and go about our duties.

We assume God's power is with us. How can it be unless we have tuned in?

I've caught myself doing this. It isn't long until my life becomes like one of the old 78 rpm records with the hole not quite in the center. How confusing everything is. I have learned the hard way to pause a little longer after I've said my part in praying, to let God speak to me. The communication goes both ways. When we listen, it completes the glorious circle in our friendship and love.

The next time you pray, remember SAL: Stop, Acknowledge Him, and Listen. Then we can go and serve.

For Listening

It's the end of another long day, Lord. I'm curled in my quiet spot telling You all about it. Thank You for listening to me. The things I say and feel may not always be right, but I am grateful for Your hearing my every word. Happy, sad, content, concerned.

How understanding and compassionate You are, dear Lord. How unquestioning is Your love. Do You laugh over my funny experiences and silly whims? Do You hurt when I share my sorrow with You? I believe You do. My love for You swells because of it.

Each time I pray, You answer and encourage me. You grant me help and strength. When trials attack my life, You, Lord, help me through. You not only listen, but buffer me from peril. You help me escape before I face more than I can bear.

When I can't feel Your presence, I launch out in faith and begin talking with You anyway. I will not doubt Your presence, for I recall the many times You have been with me.

So as I come to You with an open heart, my Lord, I quiet my thoughts. I sense Your holy presence. Then I talk. And talk. And talk!

When I'm finally talked out, You manage to put me in a place to listen—to You. In simple quiet ways, You minister to my needs and fill me with peace and joy.

Thank You, Lord, for listening to me, for helping me to hear Your still small voice.

Let us therefore come boldly unto the throne of grace, that we may obtain mercy, and find grace to help in time of need.

HEBREWS 4:16 KJV

I Love You Best

I love to have You near me, Lord. I feel secure and loved in Your presence, like a child nestled in its mother's arms. I have learned to set aside my childish ways and am pressing on toward maturity, responsibility, and sound thinking. But the little child in me still loves for You to take me in Your arms, place Your hand on my head, and bless me.

I sense Your pride for me in my accomplishments. How I treasure Your listening to me when I fail or when things go wrong. I feel Your comfort. When I grieve, I nestle within the surroundings of Your Holy Spirit and soak up Your warmth and love.

Thank You, dear Lord. How I praise You for Your timeless promise to never leave me or forsake me. I'm not a spiritual orphan wandering aimlessly.

I'm Your adopted child. I know You love Your children far more than any other of Your creation, and I love You best with all my heart and soul.

In life's celebrations, You rejoice with me, in life's challenges, You urge me on. In life's discouragements, You encourage. In the storms, You calm my fears. In my insecurities, You remind me of how much You treasure me. In victories, You are jubilant. In defeats, You are closer than ever.

You know my very being. You see my attitude, my desires, my fears, my weariness, and even my illnesses before I recognize them. How wonderful is the way You strengthen me.

Thank You for being my Good Shepherd, for nourishing and caring for me spiritually, mentally, and physically. I thank You for guiding me into safe areas and for leading me to Your living water.

You are my past, my present, my future, my life, my all.

For he hath said,
    I will never leave thee, nor forsake thee.
So that we may boldly say,
    The Lord is my helper, and I will not fear.

HEBREWS 13:5–6 KJV

Where is the key to a close relationship with Jesus Christ? Is it begging His royal presence? Reading the Bible for hours throughout the day? In sacrifice and service? Do any of these things earn merit in God's sight? Do lengthy prayers?

Christ is the key. We must allow Him to turn the lock to every room in our hearts, then fling wide the door and let Him enter. He already knows about the hidden dirt and dust bunnies in the corners. He is well aware of thoughts and actions that displease Him. We must allow Jesus not only to enter, but ask Him to bring His broom, mop, and plenty of soap!

Jesus has a way of cleansing and renewing. He can change sinful, rotten ways to a clean, sweet-smelling fragrance unto Him.

Jesus is not a mere image or a lovely picture on our wall. He is our living Savior. He wants to be our dearest Friend. When the Lord Jesus is totally welcome to every room in our lives, we will truly know His presence and be able to walk closely with Him.

GETTING TO
KNOW YOU BETTER

I delight in Your presence, O Lord. Each day I walk with You, learning to mature as a Christian. As I commune with You, I am getting to know You better. Yet I still know only a tiny morsel of Your magnificent ways.

I love You for praying for me in the Garden of Gethsemane just before You died. Although You didn't want to give Your life as a young man and take on all our sins, You were obedient to Your Father and His divine plan. I want to be willing to pay whatever cost You ask of me and to obey Your will.

I love getting to know You better. Each time I pray, I want to know more about You. When I come to You, I'm blessed by Your glorious presence, like the dawning of a new day. Your spirit refreshes and overflows on me like a soft spring rain. I tilt my head up to You and feel washed—cleaner than freshly fallen snow. How awesome to know You and Your kingdom dwell within my heart.

When I am confronted with trials, You teach me to patiently, earnestly travail in prayer. I bring my concerns and desires to You. Your Holy Spirit helps me align each one to Your perfect will.

Time and time again, You have shown me Your faithfulness. I am learning to let the worries go and thank You for the answers. When I obey, You fill me with joy and peace far greater than I can ever describe. This peace comes from You, my wonderful Lord. It keeps my mind and heart calm and relaxed as I trust in You.

My life is like a symphony as long as I am tuned to Your will. I bring my rebellious nature repeatedly and place it at Your feet. Please help me be pliable while You remold my stubborn will into something steadfast, lovely, and good, to be used by You.

What delight I have in all You do in my life, Lord! I can hardly wait to see what You have in store for me next. I trust You. My past, my present, and my future I commit to You. You are my life, my all.

Let us acknowledge the Lord;
>   let us press on to acknowledge him.
As surely as the sun rises,
>   he will appear;
>   he will come to us like the winter rains,
like the spring rains that water
>   the earth.

HOSEA 6:3 NIV

Your Yoke

Now that I have given You my all, Lord Jesus, Your yoke fits perfectly. Thank You for it and for teaching me gentleness and humility by wearing it. In doing so, I find peace and rest. You show me how we carry the loads together. This way I have twice the strength. All I need to do is follow and obey. You are the One who knows what is best.

No longer do I have to dig in stubbornly and claim my rights, because You go before me and fight those battles. Thank You, Lord, for giving me Your all. You could have called on Your angels to deliver You from the cross. Instead, You died a criminal's death. How could You have so much love?

I take up my cross and follow You, Lord. I know You help lighten the load as I trust completely in Your time, Your purpose, and Your way when troubles come. I will follow each day in Your footsteps. It doesn't matter where I stand: in poverty, wealth, fame, or glory. In everything, I will put You first and tell others about Your love.

Come to me, all you who are weary and burdened, and I will give you rest. Take my yoke upon you and learn from me, for I am gentle and humble in heart, and you will find rest for your souls. For my yoke is easy and my burden is light.

MATTHEW 11:28–30 NIV

HIS YOKE IS EASY

The Lord is my Shepherd; I shall not want.
He maketh me down to lie
In pastures green, He leadeth me
The quiet waters by.

My soul crieth out: "Restore me again,
And give me the strength to take
The narrow path of righteousness,
E'en for His own name's sake."

Yea, tho' I should walk the valley of death,
Yet why should I fear from ill?
For Thou art with me, and Thy rod
And staff comfort me still.

His yoke is easy; His burden is light,
I've found it so, I've found it so.
He leadeth me by day and by night,
Where living waters flow.

RALPH E. HUDSON, 1885

CHRIST, OUR YOKEFELLOW

We read how in ages past our ancestors used work-horses, oxen, and mules for means of transportation and heavy labor. They must not have taken long to discover that two or more animals had trouble working and pulling together. But a yoke carefully placed over a pair of the animals' shoulders helped them to pull together.

Slaves and prisoners shared yokes. In every situation, the yoke made the work stronger and more efficient.

Much later, brilliant people came up with the idea of automobiles. They invented parts of an engine that depend on each other in the same way. They found out how to make compression build up in the head by piston strokes, how to transfer the energy by rocker arms, rods, etc., to a crankshaft, then to the wheels.

Sometimes, when two people are united as one, they use the words "putting on a yoke" to express their unity. In so doing, each one is known as a yoke-fellow: an intimate associate, partner, or spouse.

When Jesus tells us to take His yoke upon us so our burden will be light, I wonder if He is offering to be our blessed Yokefellow, to lead and guide us through our daily lives.

As we let Him take control, we become one with Him. It is amazing how much easier our burdens become.

My Friend

What a wonderful gift You have given me, Father, in my dear friend. Thank You for her! In good times and bad she is there. She is a loving friend when I am at my best or my worst. In adversity, she is loyal. She rejoices with me in my gladness. She sheds tears and prays for me in my sorrows. I am so grateful for her, Lord.

Thank You for how You gave me my friend. It happened as though You planned it all along. I rejoice that she needs me, too. Thank You for showing me how to be kind and compassionate and alert to my friend's concerns and needs. When we get together, I talk and she listens, then she talks and I listen.

When I err, thank You for her forgiveness. When I do things right, thank You for her smile. She is a friend I can share my deepest secrets with. Hers are buried deep within my well of prayers, not to be revealed to anyone other than You. I praise You, Lord, for my friend, my sister in Christ.

A friend loveth at all times, and a brother is born for adversity.

PROVERBS 17:17 KJV

And now these three remain: faith, hope and love. But the greatest of these is love.

1 CORINTHIANS 13:13 NIV

THE PRICELESS FRIEND

Searching the world for riches,
Possessing wealth or fame,
Cannot fill the void within us:
Our heart, alone, in pain.

To find a friend who loves us,
Through weather foul or fair,
A friend who's like a brother,
We know is always there.

A friend is far more priceless
Than jewels, wealth, or fame,
Someone who warms heart and soul,
And through the years remains.

MY PRAYING FRIEND

When I dialed her phone number, Father, I knew my friend would already be armored to do battle in prayer for me. Not only did she pray, she fasted and prayed! What a dear and loving friend. Thank You for her.

More than once she has dropped everything so we could talk and pray together. Help me also to be keenly aware; to stop immediately and pray together with others for their needs right at the time.

How precious are our praying friends, Father. Truly, they make up Your kingdom. Thank You for hearing each earnest prayer and answering according to Your loving will. I think these prayer warriors must be a pleasure for You to watch and hear.

May I be a worthy prayer warrior in Your eyes, so Your greatness and power may be revealed and wonderful results follow. May I be there for my dear friend when she needs my love and prayers.

GOODNESS

GOODNESS

How can I ever keep up with all the good You do for me, God? Again and again, You come to my aid. You always know what I need, even before I ask.

How tender and sure Your goodness. When I need a friend, You send one who is loving and true. When I seek advice, You provide it in Your Word.

Thank You for how You remind others to pray for me when I don't even know they are doing so.

You bless me with my spouse. Children fill my quiver. How could I be more favored?

When I fall, You are there to pick me up. When I'm weak, You are strong for me. When I'm in trouble, You help me through. When I am sorrowful, You console me. Thank You for being so good.

How can I repay You, Lord? I will spread Your goodness to others, in Jesus' name.

And the LORD passed by before him, and proclaimed, The LORD, The LORD God, merciful and gracious, long-suffering, and abundant in goodness and truth, Keeping mercy for thousands, forgiving iniquity and transgression and sin. . . .

EXODUS 34:6–7 KJV

I will extol thee, my God, O king;
and I will bless thy name for ever and ever.
Every day will I bless thee;
and I will praise thy name for ever and ever.
Great is the LORD, and greatly to be praised;
and his greatness is unsearchable.
One generation shall praise thy works to another,
and shall declare thy mighty acts.
I will speak of the glorious honour of thy majesty,
and of thy wondrous works.
And men shall speak of the might of thy terrible acts:
and I will declare thy greatness.
They shall abundantly utter the memory
of thy great goodness,
and shall sing of thy righteousness.

The LORD is righteous in all his ways,
and holy in all his works.
The LORD is nigh unto all them that call upon him,
to all that call upon him in truth.

My mouth shall speak the praise of the LORD:
and let all flesh bless his holy name
for ever and ever.

PSALM 145:1–7, 17–18, 21 KJV

BECAUSE OF
YOUR GOODNESS

In spite of me, Lord,
    You accomplish many miracles.
In spite of my thoughtlessness and failures,
    You still use me to glorify You in helping others.
Thank You for being patient with me.

Through me, Lord,
    You reach out to those around me who are
hurting, to those who need You.
Because of the times I am willing to listen to You,
    You are able to accomplish miracles in others.
Thank You for helping me learn to listen.

Because of Your goodness, Lord, and Your love,
    You have put wings to my prayers and
cleats on my shoes,
        to give me speed and leverage in serving You.
Because of Your goodness,
    You have given me Your speed
        and sureness in the tough times of life.
Thank You, Lord.

How beautiful on the mountains are the feet
    of those who bring good news,
who proclaim peace,
    who bring good tidings,
who proclaim salvation,
    who say to Zion, "Your God reigns!"

When a man's ways are pleasing to
    the LORD,
he makes even his enemies live at peace with him.
Better a little with righteousness
    than much gain with injustice.
In his heart a man plans his course,
    but the LORD determines his steps.

ISAIAH 52:7,

PROVERBS 16:7–9 NIV

FOR TODAY

I look back upon this day, Lord, and I thank You for being with me. When I awoke this morning, I felt You near, urging me to be positive and look for the good in things. Through the day, You reminded me to seize the moments and use them to do Your will. When weariness set in, thank You for helping me press forward, be responsible, and not put things off.

Someone crossed my path. He needed an encouraging word and a prayer offered up for help. Thank You for urging me to be alert and tuned to hear and recognize Your voice.

Later today, You calmed my heart when hard feelings could have brewed. You sealed my lips and changed my stubborn ways to patience and kindness. Thank You for helping me love and forgive.

It's evening now. I cannot take this day back; it is gone forever. The good and the bad, Lord. Thank You for it all. I look toward a new day tomorrow in You. Let me seize it for Your glory.

In Jesus' name. Amen.

This is the day which the LORD hath made; I will rejoice and be glad in it.

PSALM 118:24 KJV

Daniel. . .went into his house; and his windows being open in his chamber toward Jerusalem, he kneeled upon his knees three times a day, and prayed, and gave thanks before his God.

DANIEL 6:10 KJV

HOW GOOD HE IS TO ME

I love to sing of Christ my King,
Who died on Calvary,
For ev'ry day along the way
How good He is to me!

He makes the night of sorrow bright,
And causes cares to flee;
He makes me glad when I am sad,
How good He is to me!
He builds above, where all is love,
A home which mine will be;
There I shall rest with all the blest,
How good He is to me!
So with a song I'll go along,
Till I my Savior see,
That souls may know where'er I go
How good He is to me!

How good He is to me,
This friend who made me free!
Each call He heeds, fills all my needs;
How good He is to me!

J. P. DENTON, 1916

ANSWERED PRAYERS

I prayed to You, dear Lord, to bless and help me as I worked for You. I sought You out time after time during my daily tasks and asked for You to keep me from wrong and disaster. To my amazement, You answered my prayers!

Why do I feel so surprised when miracles happen? More than lack of faith, I simply marvel at Your works, wisdom, and knowledge. Thank You, Lord.

The next time I anxiously call on You, please help me remember all You have done. In the meantime, right here, right now, I praise You again for answers to my prayers.

"Because he loves me," says the LORD,
    "I will rescue him;
I will protect him, for he acknowledges my name.
He will call upon me, and I will answer him;
I will be with him in trouble,
    I will deliver him and honor him.
With long life will I satisfy him
    and show him my salvation."

PSALM 91:14–16 NIV

IN ALL THINGS

I will praise You, O Lord, and bless Your holy name with all my being. I will honor You and forget not all You have done for me. No matter what has happened in the past or what lies ahead, still will I praise You.

Day in and day out will I sing of Your wonders and grace. Every chance I have, I will tell others what You do in my life. How great You are, O Mighty God! You are greatly to be praised! In all things, whether good or bad, still will I praise You. Your merciful kindness and wisdom go beyond my own limited reasoning. Because of this, I trust You completely.

I will tell my children and my grandchildren of all Your wonders. May they pass Your stories down through the generations. I will think continually of Your glorious ways. Because of how You bless me, Your good news will spread to those around me.

I offer my praise to You with hands and heart. Blessed be Your name, O Lord. Amen.

Life is so frail, dear Lord, a whisper of time. How long will I have to serve You? A few years? Months? Weeks? Perhaps You will leave me here for a long time. Whatever the case, I will bless You each precious day, making these moments fruitful by obeying You.

Thank You for my life. As long as I live, help me to bloom wherever You plant me. May I bring forth a sweet fragrance unto You.

When clouds roll in and rains descend upon me, I will shine through, wafting Your fresh perfume on the breeze. At all times, I will hold an unwavering trust in You.

I long to be Your hands and Your feet, dear Lord. Grant me patience when the paths get rough. Help me to use these years in the best way for You and not to squander them on needless, wasteful things.

Someday, I look forward to being in heaven with You. Thank You, Lord, that my life here on earth is only the beginning of my adventure through eternity.

One thing I ask of the LORD, this is what I seek: that I may dwell in the house of the Lord all the days of my life, to gaze upon the beauty of the LORD and to seek him in his temple.

PSALM 27:4 NIV

Father, thank You for my family and for the love that flows between us. We are all so different yet each constantly bridges the gaps and relates to one another.

The precious gift of my family comes from You. Thank You for reminding me never to take them for granted and for nourishing my family's love so we remain close.

When things become strained among any of us, I praise You that I can take each loved one to You and ask for help and wisdom. I never cease to be amazed at the way You give insight so I can see things from my other family members' points of view.

Thank You for the holidays, birthdays, barbecues, and picnics. Thank You, too, for the quiet one-on-one walks and talks. Some of these I will cherish for years to come.

My family isn't perfect, but I don't love them for perfection. I love them in spite of their faults. I love them because they are my family, planned for me before we ever came into being. Thank You, Father, for each one.

Finally, all of you, live in harmony with one another; be sympathetic, love as brothers, be compassionate and humble.

I Peter 3:8 NIV

Our Baby

I shall never forget that first cry. The nurse lays my newborn in my arms. Excitement fills the air. All is well. I cry. My husband gazes on with pride. Thank You, Father, for our baby.

A nurse brings our baby back, cleaned up, wrapped in a soft blanket. All is quiet. I talk with our child as we finally get to gaze at one another. How beautiful. We have known each other for nine months. But this is new. Can I meet my child's needs, Lord? Thank You for helping already.

I open the swaddling wraps. I gaze at the tiny fingers and toes. I drink in my little one's searching eyes. Then I pull my cherished, tiny offspring to my breast.

Thank You, Lord, for this phenomenal gift.

Our Children

The house rumbles with laughter and tussles. I hurry to keep up with it all. They are a heritage that comes from You. These bursts of energy in various sizes and personalities are like arrows in a warrior's hands.

I call on You for wisdom. Each day I thank You for guidance in handling different situations. Thank You, Lord, for how You help me teach our children about Your love. I treasure Your leading as I share Your lessons with them while we go about our activities at home, when we share walks, as we pray together at bedtime and rise each morning to face a new day.

My husband and I have dedicated our lives and these children to You, Lord. I know for sure Your hand is and will be upon them throughout their entire lives.

I write Your words on plaques, pictures, and on our doorposts that, "As for me and my household, we will serve the Lord" (Joshua 24:15 NIV).

These commandments that I give you today are to be upon your hearts. Impress them on your children. Talk about them when you sit at home and when you walk along the road, when you lie down and when you get up. Tie them as symbols on your hands and bind them on your foreheads. Write them on the doorframes of your houses and on your gates.

DEUTERONOMY 6:6–9 NIV

OUR TEENAGE CHILDREN

The music, hair, and clothes have changed, Lord. The children within have not. One day our teenagers feel one way, the next day it's entirely different. I feel like a yo-yo on roller skates! At times I don't know how to respond.

Thank You for placing Your protecting arms around our teenagers. Thank You for caring about their music and their hectic lifestyles. Thank You,

especially, for caring about their hearts. When I am unable to get through to them, I'm grateful You are with them.

Sometimes I fear for our kids. This is when I praise You for assurance that You are there working things together for their good.

Thank You for being with us through the joys and tears, for promising me that as we train up our children in the way of God, when they grow older, they will not depart from You.

During the shaky times, I'm thankful for these perfect gifts, our kids, that came from You. They change. You do not. You, Lord, are steadfast and sure. They will be able to come to You and depend on You anytime. You understand their needs when I'm struggling to do so. Thank You for filling gaps of communication and for hearing my every prayer for them.

I realize now that I don't have to go through the changes with my teens. Instead, I'm learning to let go of the yo-yo ways and remain steady and true so our kids can depend on me and my relationship with You. In all my ways, I'll follow You, Lord. I'll love and try to understand them the same way You love and understand me.

Thank You for helping me never compromise the standards You have set for me. I praise You for cautioning me to be kind and generous, honest and open, clean-minded and wise in speech. Thank You for strength as I strive to be a good example.

When our precious teens rebel, I praise You for help and protection for them. Thank You for being their Good Shepherd. During the times I can't seem to do anything right in their eyes, I cling to You for guidance, comfort, and reassurance. Most of all, thank You, Lord, for helping make things right when I falter.

You remind me that during these rebellious times, our teens are trying to find their own way. Thank You for helping me let go so they may search out their own personal relationship with You, so You can deal directly with them and lead them in the ways You want them to go. You, not I, are the Lord of their lives. Your plans are sure and true.

I stand back. I marvel at the wondrous miracles You perform in each of these teenager's lives. Then I praise and thank You for all You do.

Train a child in the way he should go, and when he is old he will not turn from it.

PROVERBS 22:6 NIV

ANSWERING MOTHER'S PRAY'R

While toiling in the field of time,
To keep my record fair,
I feel this recompense sublime,
I'm answering mother's pray'r.

Whene'er I cheer the lone and sad,
Or lighten someone's care,
It gives me this assurance glad,
I'm answering mother's pray'r.

Whene'er I lead some soul away
From sin's alluring snare,
It makes me happy all the day,
I'm answering mother's pray'r.

When I console some wayworn heart,
When someone's load I share,
What happiness it doth impart,
I'm answering mother's pray'r.

I hope to join the angel band,
For mother dear is there,
That I may meet her on the strand,
I'm answering mother's pray'r.

L. G. DOCKERY, 1916

I watch in awe as my grown children go about their duties. When did they become so wise, Lord? I must have done some things right. My sons and daughters-in-law are a blessing. Thank You for the love they have for each other and for us, their parents.

I hear our sons and daughters-in-law share some of the same things with their children I once taught them. I see them looking for the best in the children, continually lifting them up and praising their efforts, even as I did and do. How wonderful.

Although our sons are grown, Lord, they are still our kids. So are their wives and children. Thank You for reminding me to still look for the good in all of them and to encourage them. Each day, I pray for You to give them help and strength. I ask Your loving protection to surround them, molding them to Your will.

Thank You for nudges to do and say things or to stay quiet. I gratefully lean on Your wisdom while You show me how to be a blessing as a parent of our grown kids who still need lots of love.

Be kind and compassionate to one another, forgiving each other, just as in Christ God forgave you. Be imitators of God, therefore, as dearly loved children and live a life of love, just as Christ loved us and gave himself up for us as a fragrant offering and sacrifice to God.

EPHESIANS 4:32, 5:1–2 NIV

APPRECIATING THE AGED

Thank You, Father, for our aged Christians and the wisdom they share. Thank You for their steadfast prayer lives that help carry out miracle after miracle. Thank You for letting us build on their experiences, good and bad.

I praise You, too, for persons who are never ready to retire from working in Your kingdom. How beautiful are these who adopt the younger people, giving loving, nourishing care.

When I become aged, may I be one who continues to bless for many years.

My son, keep your father's commands and do not forsake your mother's teaching. Bind them upon your heart forever; fasten them around your neck. When you walk, they will guide you; when you sleep, they will watch over you; when you awake, they will speak to you. For these commands are a lamp, this teaching is a light, and the corrections of discipline are the way to life.

PROVERBS 6:20–23 NIV

EALING

How I praise You, Lord, for physical healing. If it weren't for You, I might have perished in my illness. I did not forget Your teaching. I clung to Your promises for help.

You have granted me a new lease on life. I feel these years are a gift from You that I must use carefully under Your direction. I am Yours, my Lord. Thank You for healing me.

You didn't heal me because of my great faith. My faith wasn't great at all. You touched my failing body when I weakly stretched out one hand to You. It was not a great demonstration, just Your quiet, steady strength. You touched me with healing in Your wings.

Thank You, Lord, for having mercy on me in my weakness and delivering me from my illness. Thank You for feeding and strengthening me spiritually as well as physically during my recovery.

When I tell others of Your mighty works, some do not believe me. Others draw strength from what I share. Their faith grows. As long as I live, I will praise and serve You, Lord, for You are my strength and my life.

Healing the
Hurting Heart

Thank You, Father, for healing my hurting heart. You took my turmoil and turned it into triumph. You gave me life anew with joy and made me whole.

Once my heart was crushed with grief. My mind spun uncontrollably. I couldn't focus on a logical thought. Nightmares kept me from sleeping. During the day, I could barely stay awake. I was so hurt I wanted to shut out the world. I wanted to die. But I knew this was against all You had taught me.

I cried out to You for relief. You came. Your Spirit visited me and anointed me. You healed my broken heart and set me free from my emotional pain. You comforted me as I gave each injury of my soul to You. You forgave my sins and helped me to forgive others.

Thank You for how You lifted my spirit of heaviness. I praise You for replacing the dark ashes of my past with beautiful new joy in You. You anointed me with the oil of gladness and took away my mourning. You placed a garment of praise on my shoulders in place of a spirit of despair.

Thank You, Father. Through Your presence, Your Word, and Christian loved ones, You helped me rebuild my life into something good and victorious. You gave me back a zest for living. Thank You for planting my feet on Your solid rock. I praise You for using my heartaches and trials to teach me wisdom, empathy, and compassion.

How wonderful is Your lovingkindness. Thank You for healing me so I can be strong for my loved ones and family for generations to come.

You are my great and mighty God. You are the Lord of Hosts. How wise are Your counsel and miraculous works. Dear Father, You see my every need.

Praise You, O God. Praise You for taking my turmoil and turning it into triumph. My weeping endured the night. Because of You, my joy came in the morning!

He was despised and rejected by men, a man of sorrows, and familiar with suffering. Like one from whom men hide their faces he was despised, and we esteemed him not.

Surely he took up our infirmities and carried our sorrows, yet we considered him stricken by God, smitten by him, and afflicted. But he was pierced for our transgressions, he was crushed for our iniquities; the punishment that brought us peace was upon him, and by his wounds we are healed.

ISAIAH 53:3—5 NIV

Comfort in Mourning

I've lost my loved one, dear Lord. I thought I would be prepared, but how could I possibly be ready for something like this? It all seems so final. No more chances to share our feelings and retrieve the time, to do and say the things undone. My heart aches. Yet at the same time, I feel Your comforting presence near.

How I praise You for comfort and strength in my time of grief. Little by little, layer by layer, You are healing my heart and soul. I praise You for surrounding me with Your warm, constant presence that helps fill the void within me.

Thank You, Lord, for reminding me in Your Word about life everlasting. Because I know my dear one loved You, all isn't final. There is life beyond death where no sadness or pain exists, a life that lasts forever. Someday You will wipe away all my tears. There will be no need of a moon or stars or sun, because of Your glorious light. There will be no sickness or pain, no sin or hurt feelings. All of this will be gone, never to return!

Even though I have tears and heartache now, I thank You for Your promise that joy will come in the morning.

I realize now You are showing me it isn't my loved one I'm weeping for. It's me. Thank You, God, for Your comfort. I look forward to joining You in heaven someday and being with my loved one again. In the meantime, I know I have more to do for You here, Lord, so I will keep going on. I will serve and praise You with all my heart.

And God shall wipe away all tears from their eyes; and there shall be no more death, neither sorrow, nor crying, neither shall there be any more pain, for the former things are passed away.

In his favour is life: weeping may endure for a night, but joy cometh in the morning.

REVELATION 21:4,
PSALM 30:5 KJV

GOOD-BY NO MORE

Oft I read about a home
Where no sin nor death can come,
And I'm pressing on to that eternal shore;
Shall I see you over there,
'Mid its beauties glad and fair,
Will you meet me where
they say good-by no more?

Thro' His great, eternal love
Jesus came from heav'n above,
And our guilt upon the cruel cross He bore;
Thus He opened up the way,
To the home of cloudless day.
Will you meet me where
they say good-by no more?

Beautiful to be with God
In the ever blest abode.
Saints and angels there
His holy name adore.
Are you gladly pressing on
To the never-fading dawn?
Will you meet me where
they say good-by no more?

J. P. DENTON, 1916

HELP

I Depend on You

I have done everything I can to overcome these problems I face, dear Lord, but it hasn't been enough. Some of my efforts have made things better. Others have not helped at all. I'm frustrated, exhausted, and at the end of my rope. I wanted to keep trying, but I realize the best thing I can do now is depend on Your help. I don't know why it has taken me so long to release all these things to You, Lord. I'm thankful You have been here waiting patiently for me, ready to take charge of my life.

Thank You for helping me to stop struggling on my own, to place everything in Your hands. I felt like I was trying to paddle a boat with only one oar. You show me the right decisions to make, when to stop trying to do anything, and most of all, how to depend on You.

Now that I'm relying on You, a huge weight of responsibility has lifted from my shoulders. As I completely, unconditionally, with no reservations, place my trust in You, I feel new joy in my life.

I look forward with invigorated anticipation to how, with Your guidance, I will find a way through it all. My heart takes delight because I trust in You, my holy God. I praise You for how Your mercy toward me is like no other. Your love is eternal. I place all my trust and hope in You.

Praise be to You, O Lord! How blessed I am for trusting and obeying You! What peace I have in delighting in Your Word. Though I have never seen You, I still know and love You, Lord. In knowing and depending on You, I am free from all that worry and frustration. I'm free to experience a life of victory in You!

Now I see the goals You set before me. You have restored and built my faith. You have once again removed my worries and doubts and replaced them with Your warm, assuring love.

The adventure has begun. I note the blessings You give along the way and praise You for each one. I refuse to dwell on the negative. I fix my mind and heart on You, Lord Jesus. Thank You for keeping me in perfect peace, for my mind is stayed on You. I will continue to trust and depend on You now and always. Thank You for being the eternal Rock of my salvation.

Thou wilt keep him in perfect peace, whose mind is stayed on thee: because he trusteth in thee. Trust ye in the LORD for ever: for in the LORD Jehovah is everlasting strength.

ISAIAH 26:3–4 KJV

I Won't Worry
for the Future

Sometimes I feel overwhelmed, wondering what the future holds. Then I remember that worry and fear are not from You. I praise You, Lord, for having control of my future.

Why should I be anxious over what tomorrow or the next day brings when I'm Your child and You have my needs and best interests at heart? Thank You for caring for me, not only now but always. Thank You for caring for those I love. I trust You that now—and even someday when I leave this perishable body and join You in heaven—You will be answering my prayers for my loved ones down through the generations.

I read of how, although Abraham's faith was strong, sometimes he doubted Your promises for his future. Sometimes he created disasters by taking things into his own hands. In spite of all that, You still blessed him and Sarah in their later years with a wonderful son.

You have authority over all, so I will not worry for the future. I will trust in You with all my heart and I won't depend on my own understanding. Instead, in all my ways I'll be in tune with You and Your will to guide and direct my paths.

Thank You for the future, Lord. I praise You for going before me and making a way.

Therefore I tell you, do not worry about your life, what you will eat or drink; or about your body, what you will wear. Is not life more important than food, and the body more important than clothes? Look at the birds of the air; they do not sow or reap or store away in barns, and yet your heavenly Father feeds them. Are you not much more valuable than they?

MATTHEW 6:25–26 NIV

THE LORD IS LEADING STILL

O ye who weary and whose hearts are dreary,
Press along and fear no ill.
For hope is beaming, golden love-light streaming,
And the Lord is leading still.

He still is reigning, many battles gaining,
So be faithful evermore;
For soon with singing and with heart bells ringing,
We shall reach the other shore.

Increase the glory of the grand old story,
Follow still God's mighty Son,
Until in heaven shall the crown be given
For many battles won.

He is leading, still is leading,
Press along and fear no ill;
Arms of love enfold you, evermore uphold you,
For the Lord is leading still.

P. B. SHAW, 1916

When You were here on earth, Lord Jesus, You pleaded to Your Father for each one of us. I thank You and praise You for that. I can't imagine the agony You must have felt at that time, the tears You must have shed for our lost souls.

I lift my heart in gratefulness because I'm allowed to know You as my Savior and Lord! I long to know You better. I am awed at how anxious You are to respond each time I come to You in prayer. You are more faithful than morning. In joy and trial I can come to You. You are here with me all the time.

Each time I align myself with Your will, I'm able to bring You my needs in faith, believing. In turn, I thank You for listening intently and taking them to Your heavenly Father on my behalf.

Praise be to You, my Lord, for each answer, whether it be "yes," "no," or "wait." You know what is best for me more than I do myself. I trust Your prayers for me and through this I have indescribable peace. This is more marvelous than any human can comprehend. Your peace helps keep my mind, body, and soul at ease when I submit to You.

My prayers to You carry much power, but that power and magnitude come from You when You intercede for me to God. Thank You for all You do for me. Yours, dear Lord, are the kingdom and power and the glory forever.

I have given them the glory that you gave me, that they may be one as we are one: I in them and you in me.

May they be brought to complete unity to let the world know that you sent me and have loved them even as you have loved me.

JOHN 17:22–23 NIV

YOU GIVE ME SELF-WORTH

O Lord, my God, how majestic is Your name above all else on this earth! You created the heavens and everything that is above. You formed the mountains and scooped out the valleys. You caused the waters throughout the earth to rise and fall. You separated them and provided dry land for Earth's inhabitants. The birds of the air, the beasts in the fields, the fish that swim their paths in the seas, lakes, and rivers: You made them all. Let everything that lives praise Your holy name.

When I try to comprehend all the mighty works and power available in even one of Your fingers, when I think of how You carefully set the sun, moon, and stars in perfect order, I wonder how You can be concerned about a single being such as I. Am I only a particle of dust in Your eye? Do you really care about my every need?

Sometimes I feel worthless and insignificant. Then I think of how You knew me while I was still being formed in my mother's womb. You know every hair on my head. You know more about me than my mother or father, my mate or children. You know more of what I am like than my closest friend.

Not only do You know me, You love and care for me. For this I am deeply grateful. Because I love You, I feel You communing with me every day.

I realize I may be insignificant by myself, but to You I'm priceless. You have called me by name to do a work for You. You hear my joys and sorrows when I pray. You take my needs and my desires seriously.

I think of what I was like when You called me to serve You. I didn't show great wisdom, I never influenced a nation, neither was I born into wealth or fame. Yet You chose a simple, everyday person like me to help in a small way to carry out Your eternal plan.

Because I have become Your child, You have given me self-worth. Thank You for showing me I am important to You. I don't need to be fearful or intimidated by the "great and mighties" of this world. They are people who need Your help, just like me. All I need do is be used of You, O God. My weakness shows Your strength. My simple understanding shows Your vast knowledge and wisdom. In all I do, let me be a living example of Your power and glory.

Are not two sparrows sold for a penny? Yet not one of them will fall to the ground apart from the will of your Father. And even the very hairs of your head are all numbered. So don't be afraid; you are worth more than many sparrows.

MATTHEW 10:29–31 NIV

PASSING THE TEST

I felt tested to the limit, Lord, but through it all I knew You were there, helping, strengthening, and comforting me. I don't know why I had to struggle, but You knew the answers and I trusted You. In the fiery trials, I still put my confidence in You and obeyed. I know You and love You, my Lord.

You refined me like a precious metal. You stood nearby and watched while my impurities painfully burned away. Now, I pray, allow me to offer You a pure heart as a sacrifice of praise and thanksgiving.

Should I be required to go through further fiery afflictions, I know I will not be consumed. Your compassionate Holy Spirit will go with me. You will give me strength to pass the test and I will praise You again.

For you, O God, tested us;
    you refined us like silver.
You brought us into prison
    and laid burdens on our backs.
You let men ride over our heads;
    we went through fire and water,
but you brought us to a place of abundance.
Praise be to God, who has not rejected my prayer
      or withheld his love from me!

PSALM 66:10–12, 20 NIV

ENCOURAGING OTHERS

My mind was fixed on my own scheduled events. I found myself going along full-speed ahead. But in the midst of everything, I felt You coaxing me to call or write to a particular person. I stopped and prayed for that one. Then I had the good sense to write their name in bold letters at the top of all other plans.

I'm not always in tune enough to recognize the needs of those around me. This is why I am thankful for Your nudges, Lord.

I stole away from responsibilities for a lunch break, ate a few bites, and headed for a nearby phone. I tapped in the number. It rang. A familiar voice answered. I knew in a moment why You told me to call.

I wonder how many people feel like Job, Lord? Alone. Rejected. Misunderstood. I want to encourage them as You show me the way. Do I notice the lonely, the discouraged? What of those I know in prisons, hospitals, nursing homes? I don't always recognize the signs of their needs. Thank You for helping me see and for showing me how to encourage.

You have blessed me, Lord. You have sent people to me when I desperately needed friends. I want to show my praise and thanks by passing on some of those blessings to others. Thank You for helping me to do so.

LEARNING TO HELP

Dear Lord, thank You for the many opportunities You give me to help the less fortunate. It may be through missions, buying someone a sandwich, telling another about Jesus, paying a young person to rake the lawn, or simply saying a kind word.

I'm ashamed of the times I have criticized others when I don't know their story. Forgive me, please.

Thank You for showing me how to help in my small way. Thank You for reminding me to pray.

He sat at the fast-food patio table where he wouldn't bother anyone and blissfully ate a sandwich. His tangled mane of hair and beard matted around his shoulders. A long, ragged, grimy overcoat hung loosely over his huge, six-foot-six frame. Although the weather soared into the eighties, he clung to his coat like a security blanket.

Bravo was his name. He never appeared lonely. He chatted happily with the windows and telephone poles.

Bravo was a menace to many until one person stepped in and found help for him.

He was somebody's son or grandson. Thank You, Lord, for Your help. Thanks also for the person who helped Bravo.

~

She was strung out on something, her thin frame ill-clad. She walked the streets at midnight and in early morning hours, darting in and out of traffic. Cars honked, trying to avoid her.

She looked sadder than a lost puppy. Then someone stepped in, helped, and never gave up on her.

She was somebody's daughter or granddaughter. Thank You, Lord, for Your help. Thanks to the one who helped her.

~

Barely ten or twelve years old, he ran with a gang. Knives, guns, brass knuckles, and much more accompanied him. His eyes flashed like hardened steel. Yet if you looked deep within, you saw fear and pain.

It seemed he and the gang only belonged to each other. Didn't anyone else care? Would he even live to see a future? Then someone stepped in and helped.

He was somebody's son or grandson. Thank You, Lord, for help and thanks to the one who helped the boy.

～

She worked two jobs and survived on meager food. When she left work, she went to her car, her temporary place to sleep. She hoped to have enough money to find an apartment soon.

Someone stepped in and helped.

She was somebody's daughter or granddaughter. Thank You, Lord, for help. To the one who helped, thank you.

～

They knocked at the doors. It was easy to tell they didn't have much money. A boy and a girl. Their eyes sparkled when they asked to do odd jobs for spending money. Things weren't easy at home.

Different folks smiled and put them to work. These children are the future. Thank You, Lord, for help. To each one who helps, thank you.

How would our church manage without the helping hands? When something needs to be done, Lord, a dear person steps in and sees to it that the job is completed. You are so good. So are they.

Some jobs in the church often go unrecognized. Yet the menial tasks are ones we benefit from the most. Wonderful people dive in and clean the church, do yard work, make repairs, do plumbing, assist with bookwork, type bulletins, usher, watch babies, bring flowers, make snacks and drinks for after church, and do dishes. Thank You for them, Lord. They are priceless.

I think You have given these saints a spiritual gift: the gift of helps. Not only do they faithfully do the jobs, they carry each one out with loving, dedicated, prayerful hearts. Praise be to You and thanks to them for their labor. Bless them, I pray, and make their labors fruitful to glorify You.

Now you are the body of Christ, and each one of you is a part of it. And in the church God has appointed first of all apostles, second prophets, third teachers, then workers of miracles, also those having gifts of healing, those able to help others. . . .

Whoever serves me must follow me; and where I am, my servant also will be. My Father will honor the one who serves me.

1 CORINTHIANS 12:27–28, JOHN 12:26 NIV

Father, thank You for showing me Your sympathy when I need it the most. In my grief, I sometimes find little comfort from dear, well-meaning loved ones and friends. Their healing words soothe for a short time, but the pain still remains.

Thank You for drying my tears and holding me near, for weeping with me in my most difficult times.

Your compassion surpasses all, Lord. You know me. You feel my pain. I can almost sense Your Holy Spirit grieving on my behalf. How I praise You for understanding me so well, for acknowledging my hurts. Thank You, Father, for Your constant love, for leading me through this grief.

Soon afterward, Jesus went to a town called Nain, and his disciples and a large crowd went along with him. As he approached the town gate, a dead person was being carried out—the only son of his mother, and she was a widow. And a large crowd from the town was with her. When the Lord saw her, his heart went out to her and he said, "Don't cry."

Then he went up and touched the coffin, and those carrying it stood still. He said, "Young man, I say to you, get up!" The dead man sat up and began to talk, and Jesus gave him back to his mother. They were all filled with awe and praised God.

LUKE 7:11–16 NIV

ANGELS WHO MINISTER

Father, I thank You for giving us Your angels. I'm grateful for each one who comes from You.

Thank You for their help and protection at Your command. I praise You, for these angels are Your heavenly messengers and servants. Thank You for being their God and for being my one and only God.

And again, when God brings his firstborn into the world, he says, "Let all God's angels worship him."

HEBREWS 1:6 NIV

About 150 years ago, Jack and Nora Cooper and their sons, thirteen-year-old Jack, Jr., and ten-year-old Tom, had just moved onto their Idaho homestead. Other settlers were in the same area, but they didn't live close to one another.

Since the country was being newly settled, irrigation ditches needed to be dug, roads to be laid out. Neighbors all around chipped in part of their meager earnings toward a fund to supply the needs. Jack Cooper was appointed as steward of the county funds. He secured the monies in a can and hid it under a loose living room floorboard in his newly built log house. The women had worked together braiding rugs from old clothing to cover their bare wood floors; now the Coopers carefully placed their braided rug over the loose board.

Late fall arrived. Winter's chill already filled the air. Jack and Nora knew they had to make a trip to town for winter supplies. They would be gone two days. As much as the trip was needed, the couple hated leaving their boys alone, yet they had no choice. Jack, Jr., stood tall and strong. He would care for the livestock. Tom could feed and water the chickens and goats.

Before leaving, Jack and Nora and the boys had their usual morning prayer. Jack especially pleaded with God to send angels for their protection.

Although the morning snapped with frost, the sunny day made doing chores easy for the boys. Near dinnertime, a knock came at the door. A kind-looking man appeared weary from travel. He explained he was heading west and needed a place to stay for the night. (Welcoming people in for food and lodging for the night was customary in those days.)

The three visited during the evening, prayed together, and said good night. The boys offered the guest a bedroom next to theirs.

In the middle of the night, Jack, Jr., and Tom were awakened by muffled squeaks, crunches, and grunts. Jack quietly crept toward his bedroom door. He could barely see a man on his hands and knees, braided rug pushed back, trying to lift the board covering the can of county money.

Jack bravely thrust open the door. At the same time, the guest bedroom door also opened. A bright white light shown sharply on the startled thief. Neither Jack nor Tom knew where it came from. The intruder bolted and ran with fright.

Jack, Jr., Tom, and their guest all returned to their beds and slept with surprising ease.

Finally, morning came. The boys' parents were due to return. Jack, Jr., and Tom prepared breakfast for their guest. They ate and happily visited together. The three prayed and thanked God for a safe night. Then the stranger thanked the boys, saddled his horse, and left.

Jack, Jr., and Tom watched the kind man ride from the farm and down into a valley. As they had done so many times before with their parents, they waited to see him ride on up the next hill beyond. They continued to wait but didn't see the stranger continue up the next hill. They waited some more. Still, nothing. Finally, they ran down the hill to see if something was wrong. No one was there. The boys found tracks from the horse. They led to a patch of dirt—and stopped. No more tracks—or man.

Jack, Jr., and Tom always wondered if there really was an angel protecting them that night.

My aunt, Virginia Meitzler, told me this story she said really happened years back to friends of her ancestors. The story has been passed down through the generations.

USED BY PERMISSION
FROM VIRGINIA MEITZLER

Angels are all around us in the form of gold pins on shoulders, other kinds of jewelry and pictures, and in stores, books, poetry, and even movies.

The Bible tells us real angels are here with us. Some of us have even experienced angels working personally in our lives. The Bible also teaches we are a little lower than the angels, but God has appointed angels and us both to be servants for Him.

We must be careful that our praise does not go to the angels, but only to God who made them. Remember, the Scriptures tell us we are to put nothing or no one before God. This includes angels.

God is the Master of all. Him only are we to worship and serve.

Let's be thankful for angels, but be thankful to God who made them.

HOPE

Hope

When trials assail me and all seems to fail, You give me hope. You are my light shining through the darkness. You are my song, my inner peace and joy. All it takes from me is to switch my focus from the catastrophes to You and Your precious promises.

As I wait upon You, I become stronger and take heart. I see goodness in all You do. I praise You for Your everlasting love. You have been my hope over and over again, my Sovereign Lord. You have the power and authority to work things together for good in my life.

Since my youth, I have learned to place my confidence in You. Each year I listen and trust You more. Now I know more than ever that You are my hope, my life.

You have promised I will be secure as I trust and obey You. Because I have placed everything in You, Lord, I rest in Your protecting hands.

The next time the storms of life are upon me, I'll hold on tight and keep my gaze on You, for You are my ever-faithful Savior.

"For I know the plans I have for you," declares the Lord, "plans to prosper you and not to harm you, plans to give you hope and a future. Then you will call upon me and come and pray to me, and I will listen to you."

JEREMIAH 29:11–12 NIV

The Past

Father, I praise You for the past. I have many good memories and some bad ones. I recall the victories, the failures, the wise choices, and the mistakes.

Thank You for each one. Help me to learn and grow because of them. Forgive my shortcomings. Show me how to forgive myself. Thank You for Your lovingkindness even when I did things the wrong way. You showered Your tender mercies upon me and blotted out my sins. You cleansed me from them all.

Thank You for teaching me to learn from my mistakes, for helping me to ask forgiveness of others, and for granting me the love and strength to forgive those who wrong me. When the hurts return, I thank You for helping me turn them over to You. Through it all, I praise You as You restore the joy of my salvation.

The good memories flow through like a sweet, floral fragrance, so pleasant, so good. The times can never be retrieved, Lord. Sometimes I wish they could. I would try to do better. I praise You for them, anyway.

Hurts and bitterness fail with Your help. Thank You for how I am learning to retrieve the lively, warm fires and to leave the sad, cold ashes behind. Now when we all get together, we sit around and recall the funny and serious old times. Forgiveness lingers like a healing balm. How dear. How marvelous. Thank You, Lord.

All the way You have led me,
From Your Word, my heart did store
Precious truths You have fed me.
I'll remember, evermore.

Through trials, dark and dreary,
You stayed with me all the way.
Through victories I see clearly,
Your guidance, come what may.

What of the past still lingers?
Bitterness and strife?
Nay, for I hear You whisper,
"Think of the good in life."

THE FUTURE

Father, thank You for the future. Although there are times I feel unsure about what lies ahead, the future for me and the ones I love is in Your hands. I feel confident You will be with me through the good times and the struggles. While I obey Your Word, You will take my personal concerns to heart and bless me with what You know is best for me.

I will glorify You by committing my future plans to You. For each endeavor, I will trust You to help and direct. As I work within Your will, I know You will bless my labor with success. Thank You for helping me remember to never stray from Your leading. I praise You for strength to do right.

You, Lord, are my Shepherd. How dear You are for providing my needs, for granting me rest. How marvelous it is when You guide me and give me peace.

I love You for Your kindness and patience with me when I worry about the what-ifs. Your understanding and mercy help melt my fears. Thank You for reminding me often not to worry. Fear does not come from You. I'm in Your hands; You know my needs before I even ask.

Now I take my frustrations and anxious concerns and lay them at Your feet, dear Lord. A huge weight lifts from my shoulders as You pick them up. Thank You for taking them over once again. Through this, I thank You and praise You for all that lies ahead.

I am God, and there is none like me, declaring the end from the beginning, and from ancient times the things that are not yet done, saying, My counsel shall stand, and I will do all my pleasure.

ISAIAH 46:9-10 KJV

If You Should
Roll Out the Future

If you should roll out the future
Like a scroll across the sky,
You'd show me stories from days of old,
Give guidance none could deny.

If You should reach down Your fingertip,
And write on parchment for me
Answers to questions that tear at my heart,
And solve all life's mysteries;

Could I fathom the hidden secrets?
Would it set my heart at ease?
Or give me burdens far greater,
And increase my earnest pleas?

You show me in the Bible,
That, although I cannot see,
I have Your presence with me,
Now through eternity.

I read the answers You've given,
Your promises great and true;
Your fingertip etches deep in my heart:
"I'll truly take care of you."

Father, I praise You for the heaven You have prepared for me. I long to see the holy city, to worship in Your tabernacle. It won't be a tabernacle built by hands, but Your enveloping presence, Lord God Almighty, will be the temple.

I don't feel worthy. Thank You for covering me with Your redemptive blood so I may enter.

Will there really be no tears? No sickness? No pain? Will all believers in Christ be alive, happy, and well? Will we never thirst again, but drink from the water of life? Ah, yes! How grand it will be! Praise You, Lord.

I look forward to entering that holy city, Father. I can't imagine its beauty, the light being as a precious jasper stone, clear as crystal.

You have told me in Your Word there will be no need for a sun to shine by day, or a moon by night. For the glory of You, Father, will lighten it and Your Son, the Lamb of God, will be the light. There will be no need for lights: You will give us all we need. Neither will we have to lock the gates or doors. There shall be nothing to fear.

Best of all, You, Lord God the Father, the Son, and the Holy Spirit, the Alpha and Omega, the Beginning and the End, shall reign forever and ever!

GLADNESS ETERNAL

We shall gather beyond the river,
In the presence of Christ the giver
Of joys we have today,
And shall sing of His love eternal
With the angels of light supernal,
When the shadows pass away.

Ev'ry trouble and care will leave us,
Nothing ever again will grieve us,
When we meet Him on that day;
Ended ever will be all sorrow,
On the beautiful, sweet tomorrow,
When the shadows pass away.

We shall enter our home rejoicing,
Sweet hosannas to Jesus voicing,
Never more from God to stray;
Perfect rapture will overflow us,
For our mansions the Lord will show us,
When the shadows pass away.

Gladness eternal, wonderful gladness,
Even now is waiting thee;
Gladness and glory there with the angels,
Thro' the ages we shall share.

K. C. ROBINSON, 1916

Oh, He has prepared a glorious heaven for you!
It is already waiting for you, not merely a throne, but
steps by which to mount it. Not only a harp, but a
tune to play on it. Not only a bannered procession,
but victory which it is to celebrate.

T. DeWITT TALMAGE

I'M ON MY WAY HOME

I'm on my way home, Lord. I focus all my thoughts on You, my Light through darkness. When I finally come to heaven with You, my sadness, pain, and mourning for those gone ahead will be no more. I can't comprehend it. No sun? No moon? Not even a star will be needed to light the way! Your glorious presence will cast an iridescence that will show the way for all who believe in You. A light, pure and white. I wonder if the human eye is even able to gaze upon it.

Thank You for choosing me to come. I know it's my time and You're calling me Home. Thank You, Lord, that through Your blood I am counted worthy.

I praise You for how You forgave my sins and washed them away. I can only be pure through You, Christ Jesus. How thankful I am to belong to You. I praise You for calling me from darkness into the light. Once my heart was filled with sin. Now I am clean and set free. Thanks be to You, O Lord!

I praise You that You will share Your wonderful heavenly home with me. You are calling me. I can feel it. I'm ready to go, to step into Your lighted pathway. I'm anxious to see the love and favor in Your eyes.

The night of suffering will give way to morning. Dawn will break through. I will hear the angels sing praises. I can almost hear Your voice, dear Jesus, saying, "Welcome home, My child."

Lord, in this fast-paced, complicated world, I have mixed feelings when praying for Your return. I see much good here, yet still I long for You to come again and take me home. Heaven feels like a place I know subconsciously. Although I only read about it, I have a deep, homesick feeling within me. I long to go there.

Then I ask, "What about the lost?" There are so many loved ones and friends who need You as their Savior. Noah must have felt this way when he tried to warn the people while building the ark.

I don't want these dear ones lost. Yet as much as I care for them, I know Your love for them far surpasses mine, Lord Jesus. You must be tugging on each one's heart. Your plan and timing for Your coming is perfect. I trust You without question.

I want to see You soon. I have much to ask You. I yearn to be near You, Lord, to see You face-to-face. Oh, I wish You would step through the clouds right now like lightning cutting through the gray. Would

the mountains tremble in Your presence? Would I fall to my knees along with the many other Christians, filled with fear, awe, and reverence?

Please come, Lord. I can hardly wait for our jubilant reunion when I can see Your wonderful glory.

Jesus, even while I have never had the privilege to perceive You physically, I love You with all my heart. I know You because Your Spirit dwells within me. You are my only hope. When You return, I would be terrified had You not paid the price for my sins. There is no way I could deserve to look into Your face unless You are my Savior. I praise You for Your promise to return for Your blood-bought children.

"Soon," You say.

Come soon, O Lord. So be it in Your timing.

I will look to You, my King, my trusted Savior. "You're here. You're here, Lord Jesus!" I will cry. "I rejoice, for You're here. Praise be to You, O God!"

For now, I look toward the sky for Your return. While I'm waiting, I thank You, Lord, for helping me to keep reaching out for the lost.

No one knows about that day or hour, not even the angels in heaven, nor the Son, but only the Father. As it was in the days of Noah, so it will be at the coming of the Son of Man. For in the days before the flood, people were eating and drinking, marrying and giving in marriage, up to the day Noah entered the ark; and they knew nothing about what would happen until the flood came and took them all away. That is how it will be at the coming of the Son of Man. Two men will be in the field; one will be taken and the other left. Two women will be grinding with a hand mill; one will be taken and the other left. Therefore keep watch, because you do not know on what day your Lord will come. But understand this: If the owner of the house had known at what time of night the thief was coming, he would have kept watch and would not have let his house be broken into. So you also must be ready, because the Son of Man will come at an hour when you do not expect him.

MATTHEW 24:36–44 NIV

*J*OY

When You are the center of my life, dear Lord, I'm filled with exceedingly great joy. A joy that wells up within me to overflowing.

Troubles may assail on all sides. Circumstances may seem impossible to overcome, but joy is at the center of my being. When I am bone-tired, Your joy, Lord, is my strength.

Thank You for teaching me what is important in life. It isn't a smooth-flowing life with no trials or stress (although I long for that!). It isn't perfect happiness and plenty of riches. The important thing is to stir up goodness, kindness, peace, and joy, generated by Your Holy Spirit.

Thank You for true joy that comes from You. I can't quit telling others about this joy You give me. Your songs of praise and Scriptures flow from my heart. I fall asleep with a prayer trailing from my lips. I awaken with a hymn of praise flowing through my mind. You, Lord, are my joy and strength.

In good times and bad I have learned to praise You. As my praises soar upward to You, new continuing joy fills my heart like an artesian well. The more joy I pass on to others, the more You refill my well with unquenchable joy.

On the mountaintop when all is well, we praise You easily. But when we are forced into the valleys of despair, Your Holy Spirit still brings confidence and joy as we focus on You. My heart may ache when things go wrong—but my joy in You remains. Thanks to You, Lord: Your joy is my strength.

For the kingdom of God is not a matter of eating and drinking, but of righteousness, peace and joy in the Holy Spirit, because anyone who serves Christ in this way is pleasing to God and approved by men.

Be filled with the Spirit. Speak to one another with psalms, hymns and spiritual songs. Sing and make music in your heart to the Lord, always giving thanks to God the Father for everything, in the name of our Lord Jesus Christ.

ROMANS 14:17-18, EPHESIANS 5:18-20 NIV

But let all those that put their trust in thee rejoice: let them ever shout for joy, because thou defendest them: let them also that love thy name be joyful in thee. For thou, Lord, wilt bless the righteous; with favour wilt thou compass him as with a shield.

PSALM 5:11-12 KJV

FIND JOY

Find it in the sunshine.
Let the clouds go by.
Look, then in the roses.
Never mind the thorns.
Notice a watermelon
Hiding in the weeds.

Count the smiles you see
After facing a frown.
Pass along a kindness
To one who is sad.

Find your joy and comfort
In sweetnesses of life.
Mix sugar with the lemon.
Avoid the bitterness.

Stay in tune with the Master.
He is your strength each day.
Lift your heart to Him in song.
And you shall then find joy.

Rejoice in the Lord alway:
 and again I say, Rejoice.

PHILIPPIANS 4:4 KJV

ABUNDANT LIFE

Thank You, Lord, for giving me a joy-filled, abundant life. You do not provide for me a life that functions under the circumstances, but one that triumphs over the circumstances!

I have found a way that transcends all happiness. In You, Lord Jesus, I have more: a deep, bubbling, unquenchable, satisfying, everlasting joy and peace. Thank You, God.

Your Spirit fills my soul's well to overflowing. You supply me with Your living water. It satisfies my thirst for You day after day. It springs up and spills over onto those around me.

Thank You for saving me. Thank You for keeping me. I praise You, Lord, for filling me with Your Spirit and giving me abundant life in You.

I have come that they may have life,
and have it to the full.

JOHN 10:10 NIV

CELEBRATION

This day is a highlight for me. A time to celebrate. Thank You for making all this possible. The banquet table is set. Friends and loved ones gather from far and near.

I rejoice before You, O Lord, for You have been my joy and strength. Though there has been much work involved, on this day I rest and rejoice! I lift my praise to You in song. I clap my hands and rejoice in the triumphant victories. You, my God, are awesome. You are the Most High Lord, Creator of Heaven and Earth.

I sing more praises to You, O God, my King of kings. I honor You with praise and exalt Your name. I will tell all those around me of Your great accomplishments that cause me to celebrate. Praise You for Your mighty acts and excellent greatness.

You have blessed the work of my hands. You knew when I trudged through the wilderness of struggles and You helped me.

Because I put my trust in You, I rejoice and shout for joy. Because I love Your name, I am filled with gladness. With all my breath will I praise You, O God. Praise be the Lord!

Let us come before his presence with thanksgiving, and make a joyful noise unto him with psalms. For the Lord is a great God, and a great King above all gods. O come, let us worship and bow down: let us kneel before the Lord our maker.

PSALM 95:2–3, 6 KJV

O sing unto the Lord a new song:
 sing unto the Lord, all the earth.
Sing unto the Lord, bless his name;
 shew forth his salvation from day to day.
Declare his glory among the heathen,
 his wonders among all people.
For the Lord is great,
 and greatly to be praised:
  he is to be feared above all gods.

Let the heavens rejoice,
 and let the earth be glad;
let the sea roar,
 and the fulness thereof.
Let the field be joyful,
 and all that is therein:
then shall all the trees
 of the wood rejoice before the Lord.

PSALM 96:1–4, 11–13 KJV

SING A NEW SONG

Sing a new song unto the Lord!
Show forth His grace from day to day;
Let all the earth e'er sing His word;
He is the Life, the Truth, the Way.

Worship the Lord in holiness;
On Calv'ry's cross the Christ was raised;
God gave His Son the world to bless,
The Lord is greatly to be praised.

Let people fear the coming King,
For with His truth He'll judge the world;
The righteous shall His praises sing,
And sinners from Him will be hurled.

Sing a new song, at church, at home,
Sing of God's love so great, so sweet;
Sing of the time that soon will come,
When we shall sing at Jesus' feet.

GEORGE W. ANDERSON, 1916

LOVE

Your Love

I am so glad You love me, heavenly Father. Thank You for loving me just the way I am. I'm not all that great. I don't possess any remarkable status or money in this world. I'm just an ordinary person who wants to love and serve You.

I love You with all my heart. I'm ashamed to admit, though, that it was because You first loved me. I praise You, Father, and give You my life, for You have adopted me into Your family as one of Your own.

Thank You for having so much love that You gave Your Son who died and rose again for me. I am grateful for Jesus. He is able to bring me into Your holy presence, where I may share my little and big concerns with You. Thank You for listening to me, walking with me, and guiding me each day. You are not only my Father, You are my dearest Friend.

I praise You, Father, for the way Your love shines on me and on all of humankind. It is so wonderful how You created everything and regulate it all. Great are Your works. Great is Your love, O Father.

The One-Hundredth Sheep

How far did You search, Lord? How did You ever find me? My thoughts and speech were scrambled. My life, total destruction. I saw no way out. In order to rescue me did You search through frightening and sinful situations where angels would fear to tread?

I was lost, but You found me. I was worthless, but You saw promise in me. I was afraid to change, but You cut through my fear. I was alone, but You sent a Christian to comfort and love me. Thank You, Lord Jesus.

I feel like the lost one-hundredth sheep You finally found and forgave. Then You placed me in Your sheltering fold.

Over and over again, I had tried to climb out of the bottomless pit I had gotten myself into. My Christian friend kept reminding me, "Nothing is impossible, when you place all your trust in God."

Thank You, Lord, for searching me out and saving me. And thank You for my Christian friend. Thank You for planting my feet upon Your solid rock. I praise You for forgiving my sins and providing me a joyous, new life in You. Thank You for seeing me as a sheep worth everything to You.

What do you think? If a man owns a hundred sheep, and one of them wanders away, will he not leave the ninety-nine on the hills and go to look for the one that wandered off? And if he finds it, I tell you the truth, he is happier about that one sheep than about the ninety-nine that did not wander off. In the same way your Father in heaven is not willing that any of these little ones should be lost.

MATTHEW 18:12–14 NIV

GOD'S LOVE
NEVER GIVES UP

About ten years ago my mother and father stepped through our door loaded with Christmas gifts for my husband, myself, and our growing sons. One gift was a ten-inch fir tree carefully planted in a pot and adorned with dainty decorations. I love growing things and this little tree was no exception.

The following spring, I carefully planted it in our backyard, just far enough from another fir tree our son Dave planted as a Cub Scout. They would be a perfect hammock length apart, I figured, by the time my husband and I retired.

While the little tree was small, I guarded it from bicycles, balls, and jumping youngsters. I faithfully gave it water and tender loving care. The small tree miraculously survived and outgrew our boys.

Then something strange happened. The soft fir needles changed to long, coarse ones, like those of a bull pine tree. I was thrilled and enjoyed its lovely stature even more.

Ten years went by. The tree stood a majestic twenty feet tall. Winter set in. Snow and ice tore through northwest Washington like a roaring monster, seeking to destroy all in its path. The weight of the ice on the branches caused the trees all around to come crashing down. Our pine tree held up.

One morning I trudged out in the snow to check everything. Two huge branches had broken from the trunk, leaving a two-foot hole in their place. Six feet of the tree's top had given way. Huge branches from the pitiful green giant filled half the yard. I stood there and sobbed.

I knew people had lost their homes from fallen trees. I knew I should be thankful for our warmth and safety. But memories of the tiny Christmas gift from Mother and Dad (Mother had passed away since then), growing children, and strangely changing pine needles flashed through my mind.

My husband, Bob, viewed the scene with much more logic. He felt the tree would never survive, and we would have to take it out. I knew I had to be reasonable and trust his judgment.

Stayci, our daughter-in-law, came and checked it. She told me of "goop" that could seal the injured areas so the tree wouldn't lose all its sap. I immediately went to work. The only "goop" I could find was black, but it would have to do. Friends and neighbors helped us remove broken branches and cut up wood for the neighbor's fireplace.

After we finished the pruning, gooping, and clearing, I did what may sound silly. Alone in our yard I carefully placed my hands on the huge hole in the trunk and thanked God for our tree. I asked Him to help it survive.

After a few months, Bob checked the tree again. He decided not to cut it down, because he "didn't want any more tears."

Two years passed. New growth kept coming on. One day when I was working in the yard, I noticed bark actually pushing its way through the still-black goop I had sprayed on the tree after the storm. The tree was restoring itself. Needless to say, I thanked God for answering my prayer.

The scars are there. The top is gone. But to me, it is beautiful and healthy. The birds nest in its branches. Near the broken area hangs my husband's birthday gift, a gazebo-type bird feeder used every day by our feathered population. I love to sit under the tree while I write. I smell the sweet pine fragrance, better than any air freshener. Life is still there. I'm glad I didn't give up.

Isn't that the way it is with God? When we're shattered, broken, and bruised from the storms in life, He's there picking up the broken pieces, mending us, and helping us grow again.

I wonder if the bark pushing through will grow into a beautiful burl. I wonder what beauty God will create from our injuries.

Isn't it wonderful that He never gives up on us?

And the god of all grace, who called you to his eternal glory in Christ, after you have suffered for a little while, will himself restore you and make you strong, firm and steadfast.

1 PETER 5:10 NIV

THE POWER
OF GOD'S LOVE

A cruel scar showed on a nearby tree,
Fallen branches from storm and ice.
Its trunk was bare along one side,
Gashed where branches were sliced.

Slow years slipped over the emerald pine,
Fresh growth began to sprout once more
New branches, the tree triumphantly raised,
Far more lovely than ever before.

Each deep scar tells of battles won,
The tree is changed forever by pain.
Its beauty is filled with character,
Lessons in healing remain.

A cruel scar showed on a fallen soul,
Broken feelings from ice and storm,
A heart was breaking deep inside,
A trembling life, beaten, torn.

Years slipped by, God tenderly touched
And healed the broken heart once more.
He made the soul both strong and sure,
Far more lovely than ever before.

Each cruel scar tells of battles won.
The soul will never be the same.
God brought needed character,
To praise and glorify His name.

SHOWERS OF BLESSINGS

I have searched for You, Lord, in my parched and exhausted life. My soul gasps for Your living water. I praise You as You refresh me with a cool, clear rain from heaven, Your holy Word.

As I read my Bible, Your words gently quench my thirst. Thank You for when You water and nurture the seeds of my spiritual life and make them mature so I may produce good spiritual fruit for You.

I look up toward heaven and let You bathe my face, my whole being. I taste Your sweet waters and know they are good. You wash and cleanse me, making me white as pure snow. New energy surges through me.

Thank You for showering me with overflowing blessings. My whole life becomes a fountain. Its water overflows to the parched and weary ones about me. How blessed are You, my Lord! How sweet and life-giving is Your love!

I will send down showers in season;
there will be showers of blessing.

You my sheep, the sheep of my pasture, are people,
and I am your God, declares the Sovereign Lord.

EZEKIEL 34:26, 31 NIV

MARRIAGE—HER

The organ is playing, Lord. I stand at the sanctuary doorway, my arm locked in my father's. I tremble with excitement and uncertainty as I prepare to meet my husband-to-be and exchange our vows.

What lies ahead? Will he love me forever? I know I will him. Will we have many years together? God, please lead and bless us. Help us keep You first in our lives. Show us how to love with a true, selfless, undying love. Help me be a good wife and helpmate.

Thank You, Lord, for helping us prepare for this day. We have spent a lot of time praying together for Your will in our lives. Thank You for reminding us to build our marriage on You, a sure foundation.

We will cling to Your many promises and thank You for being with us in the good times and the bad. When we are weak, I already thank You for making us strong.

The Bridal March begins. My beloved turns and gazes at me with love and pride. Dad and I step forward. With a kiss on the cheek and a squeeze of my hand, Dad lovingly releases my arm and guides me toward the second man I love. A new life is about to begin for the two of us, a life where we will become one.

Thank You, Lord for our love and our marriage. We kneel to pray, asking You to be the head of our new home. Thank You for our future together, in You.

MARRIAGE—HIM

The organ is playing, Lord. I stand at the altar so nervous I'm shaking in my shoes. I wonder if my best man will have to hold me up. My head spins with excitement and uncertainty as I prepare to receive my wife-to-be and exchange our vows.

What lies ahead? Will she love me forever? I know I will her. God, please lead us and bless us. Help us keep You first in our lives. Show us how to love with a true, selfless, undying love. Help me be a good husband and provider.

Thank You, Lord, for helping us prepare for this day. My love and I have spent a lot of time praying together for Your will for us. Thank You for helping us build our marriage on You, a strong foundation.

We will hang on to Your promises. We thank You for being with us through the good and the tough times. If we are tempted to not be at our best, bring us where You want us to be.

I hear the Bridal March. I turn and gaze at her. Lord, she is so beautiful. Her father kisses her on the cheek and guides her toward me. My beloved and I are about to begin a new life and become one.

Thank You, Lord, for our love and our marriage. We kneel to pray, asking You to be the head of our new home. Thank You for our future together, in You.

Your Call to Love

Thank You, Jesus, for calling me to love. Not a love because of what others do, but an unconditional, everlasting love. I can only have the capacity to love like this when it comes from You.

You not only show me how to care for the lovely but for those who aren't so lovable. Thank You for showing me how to take a firm stand for what is right and for helping me to disagree with those who do wrong, yet still care about them.

I'm grateful for Your urging me again and again to pray for the salvation of those who do wrong, even when they hurt me. But thank You for granting me the strength not to just stand there and take mistreatment. I know it isn't Your will for me to be a doormat. Help me leave the judgment of others to You.

Thank You for reminding me to love those closest to me, to cherish and treasure them and not take them for granted.

I can speak with eloquence and pass out all sorts of good advice. Still, I must have a true, sincere love.

I can have all sorts of spiritual gifts, but they are worthless unless my love is pure and selfless. I can give all sorts of gifts and help others, but they mean nothing without Your unconditional love.

Father, You have called me to love. Let it come from You, I pray. Let me love, not envy. Let me listen and care, not brag or put down. Help me look past the faults and see others' needs. Let me look for the good in them. Help me bear the griefs, share the dreams, hope the hopes, and see past the faults of those who need love.

When my patience is stretched, help my love never fail. Fill my cup with Your spirit-filled love until I overflow. Then, like a well within me, let me give that love. And give it. And give it. The more I give, the more You place within me.

Since this love isn't conjured up within me, it can only come from You, Lord. I thank You and praise You for Your call to love.

When love is given, so comes the joy.

CHRISTIAN LOVE

Lonely hearts long for love,
While each day rushes by.
Weary souls have no love,
Yet each day rushes by.
Take a smile, pass it on,
When you go hurrying by.
Say a prayer, do a deed,
For each day rushes by.

PEACE

PEACE

Though troubles surround me and stress invades my life, I revel in the presence of Your comforting Holy Spirit. It is here I find a deep, satisfying peace. How I praise You for it, Lord.

All I must do is obey Your will and cast each care upon You in faith, believing. There You grant me peace, a peace You wanted me to have all along had I only listened sooner.

My methods of problem solving, the wisest counsel, even a tranquil, quiet place can't offer the peace You give. A peace of body, mind, and soul.

When these trials surround me, Lord, I resolve not to be troubled or afraid. Instead, I praise You for taking hold of each situation and helping me solve my problems.

My heart fills with hope and peace; I trust in You. Peace flows through me like a warm, soothing balm, powerful and sure.

In You I believe, my Lord. In You I trust. I am totally confident You are able to keep safe all I commit to You until You return to take me to heaven.

You are just and mighty. You are my peace. You quiet my heart and make me confident of Your care each day. I center my thoughts on You, Lord. In You I live safely and without fear.

Day and night I will heed Your Word and treasure Your peace within my heart and mind. A peace that warms and soothes like a sunrise and flows through me as a gentle stream. A peace that floods and washes over the trials and stress with powerful, cleansing waves of righteousness. Peace, victorious and sure! Thank You, God, for it!

Peace I leave with you; my peace I give you. I do not give to you as the world gives. Do not let your hearts be troubled and do not be afraid.

JOHN 14:27 NIV

Be careful for nothing; but in every thing by prayer and supplication with thanksgiving let your requests be made known unto God. And the peace of God, which passeth all understanding, shall keep your hearts and minds through Christ Jesus.

PHILIPPIANS 4:6-7 KJV

SEASONS

Bob and I broke away from responsibilities and took a drive to our favorite place, the ocean, for a couple of days. After a brief night's sleep, I awakened early.

No matter how tired I am, I can't resist waking before dawn and walking out to a nearby jetty. This morning was no different. I quietly slipped into warm clothes and shoes. Bob already knew where I would go. Before long, my strides lengthened and quickened. I approached the pier.

Responsibilities had been crashing in on my life harder than the breakers hitting the huge rocks before me. I watched the waves roll in. They crashed, sprayed, and flowed out over and over in rhythmic patterns, then prepared to do it again.

"Lord, why must I be stretched so thin? I don't think I can handle it all much longer," I whispered.

The sun peeked above the ocean and reflected its rays across the waves.

Peace, be still, I felt God whisper on the wind. *Look at the tide change. It's going out now. To everything*

there is a time and a season. The hard toil won't last for-
ever. In the meantime, today—rest.

God reminded me to praise Him while I
watched the waves recede. Cold air rushed about me,
but warmth filled my being. His presence comforted,
assured.

"Thank You, God, for the seasons," I prayed.
I turned, set a quick pace, and headed toward rest,
a hot cup of tea, and my waiting beloved. I had
been blessed.

To every thing there is a season, and a time to every
purpose under the heaven.

ECCLESIASTES 3:1 KJV

PROMISES OF JESUS

Faithful is the One who leads the way,
Loving are the words He speaks each day;
Tender is His promise, full of cheer:
"I am always with thee, never fear."

Sorrows may beset me, ills pursue,
I can trust this Friend so kind and true.
Precious is His promise, full of grace:
"I will lead thy footsteps in life's race."

Ever at my side He walks unseen,
Mighty is the arm on which I lean;
Gracious is His promise, full of love:
"I've prepared for thee a home above."

Ev'ry precious promise cheers my soul,
All along the journey to the goal;
Words of peace and pardon, hope and love,
Bless me on the road which leads above.

WILLIAM P. DAVIS, 1916

Thank You, Father, for promising me that when I come to You I will receive rest. I am weary. I know I need a break. But the more I see what needs to be done, the more I drive myself. I am bone-tired. I can barely put one foot before the other. My body aches from weariness to the point I can't sleep. My emotions are drained. Sometimes I feel as though I am being stripped away piece by piece, wondering if I will fall apart. But in the midst of all of this, I take time to tune in to You, the Source of my strength. I take time to praise You.

I realize it isn't good for me to work this hard. Yet circumstances require my extra work for the time being. Thank You for promising me rest. You are my Light at the end of the tunnel. I have already committed all my responsibilities, my energy to You, Father. When I'm tempted to try to solve these work duties on my own, I pray for You to help me not have a particular plan in mind, for You know best.

I don't want to be like Jonah and refuse to listen. He certainly found himself in a mess. And even after

You delivered him from the great fish's belly, he went through more. I read of how the hot sun beat down on his head during his struggle until he grew faint. Finally, Jonah asked You to let him die. Instead, You provided him a way of escape.

I pray I will not be so persistent and demand to do things my way. Through my struggles, Father, help me yield to Your wise counsel as You lead me and provide the rest I so desperately need. I look forward to it and praise You, my Provider.

In the meantime, thank You for helping me complete my work with a job well done. I praise You, Father, for my second wind of energy. The joy I find in You is my strength.

REST AT LAST

Lord Jesus, thank You for this rest that has finally come. It is only a short, unexpected time in my own backyard, but to me it is a haven. I am so grateful for it. My weary heart cried out for You to rescue me and give me rest. How merciful and loving You are for answering my prayers.

You must have been weary, too, when You walked this earth, Lord. Did God provide times and ways for You to break away, rest, and pray? Thank You for helping me remember to take time with You, the Source of my strength. I read how You, Lord, frequently took time and communed with Your Father. Thank You for being my example, my Savior.

This quiet time in my yard is so tranquil. My family moves about inside, quietly, protectively. I'm grateful they sense my needs. I can hear the flutter of birds in the trees.

I sink into the lawn chaise and close my eyes. I read Your precious Word. After a time, my Bible slips from my hands and falls gently to the green carpet of lawn. I feel no sense of time. Instead, I sleep and pray; read, sleep, and pray some more. My head clears. My perspective on decisions to be made comes into focus. My muscles and bones feel stronger. Yet still I remain, absorbing Your Holy Spirit and feeding on Your Word.

What sweet rest. Thank You, Lord. Tomorrow I begin work anew. Until then, I lay all aside, return to enjoy my family, and continue to rest.

Come to me, all you who are weary and burdened, and I will give you rest.

MATTHEW 11:28 NIV

SERVICE

THANK YOU FOR CALLING ME

Father, how did You look down and see me among all these people and decide what work You especially would have me do? Thank You for Your calling.

I get so excited about all You've done, I can't keep still. I want to tell everyone about Your measureless love and what You have done for me.

Telling others of Your love doesn't make me special. All the glory goes to You, my Lord. I'm not serving You according to my plans. It's because You chose me. You gave me a calling and granted me Your sacred trust.

Sometimes the responsibilities of Your calling are overwhelming and frightening. Who am I? Only one little insignificant person in this great big world. But I must tell all who will listen of the marvelous things You do, the awesome lessons You teach in Your Word. When my time is slim and my energy low, I pray for You to multiply my efforts as You did the loaves and fishes. So much can be accomplished for You. Thank You for continuing to help me remember to view my interruptions as opportunities to be a blessing.

Thank You for calling me. No matter the cost, help me always to be a servant You can be pleased with. May You look at me someday and say, "Well done, My good and faithful servant."

But now, this is what the Lord says—
    he who created you, O Jacob,
    he who formed you, O Israel:
"Fear not, for I have redeemed you;
    I have called you by name;
    you are mine.
When you pass through the waters,
    I will be with you;
    and when you pass through the rivers,
    they will not sweep over you.
When you walk through the fire,
    you will not be burned;
    the flames will not set you ablaze.
For I am the Lord, your God,
    the Holy One of Israel, your Savior. . . .
You are precious and honored
    in my sight. . .
    because I love you."
"You are my witnesses,"
    declares the Lord,
"and my servant whom I have chosen,
    so that you may know and believe me
        and understand that I am he."

ISAIAH 43:1–4, 10 NIV

Have you come to a fork in your road of life? Do you feel God's call to serve? Do you recognize His voice and know it is Him? Simply wait on Him and say, "Yes."

Don't ponder the what-ifs or whys, neither question your abilities. Don't worry about timing or the future. Test the calling to be sure it is of God. When you know it is Him, simply tell Him, "Yes."

When the mighty winds blow, He will miraculously place them at your back. When the floods begin to rage, He may tell you to keep paddling in faith, believing, while He calms the seas.

God's calling is sure. We don't have to worry about making a way. If it is His will, He works all things out in His own perfect way and timing.

He calls us through, around, over, and under to serve. No foe can stop us, no poverty can starve us, no evil can diminish His call. For He has a glorious plan!

So, just say, "Yes."

The eyes of your understanding being enlightened; that ye may know what is the hope of his calling. . . .

EPHESIANS 1:18 KJV

HEAR THE CALL

I hear Jesus call to me,
"There's work for you to do."
I see many hurting souls.
"Come, show them life anew."

"You must reap the harvest,
Of those who search for Me."
I still hear Him calling:
"From sin I'll set them free."

God, why must I be the one?
Why are You calling me?
"Because they need your help, My child."
"Then here am I, send me."

How, then, can they call on the one they have not believed in? And how can they believe in the one of whom they have not heard? And how can they hear without someone preaching to them? And how can they preach unless they are sent? As it is written, "How beautiful are the feet of those who bring good news!"

ROMANS 10:14-15 NIV

MAKE ME A PEBBLE

What do You see in me that I could be used to serve You, Lord? I feel honored that You called me. Whatever You ask of me, I will do.

You are my Lord. I will not fear Your call, for You know me completely and recognize what I can do for You.

I praise You and say "yes" to Your call. I know You are with me to help and guide. I'm not a rock like Peter, but I can be a little pebble that serves You. I am Your child and You are my God. Thank You for accepting my strengths and weaknesses.

How exciting it will be in this venture as I obey Your call and see great things happen in Your name!

Take me, Lord. Use me. Let me glorify Your name. Whatever You ask of me, I will do.

And he said unto me, My grace is sufficient for thee: for my strength is made perfect in weakness. Most gladly therefore will I rather glory in my infirmities, that the power of Christ may rest upon me. Therefore I take pleasure in infirmities, in reproaches, in necessities, in persecutions, in distresses for Christ's sake: for when I am weak, then am I strong.

2 CORINTHIANS 12:9–10 KJV

WORKING FOR THE MASTER

I would be a faithful worker
In the service of the Lord;
I would make some sad heart gladder
By a kind and loving word;
I would carry joy and sunshine
To the darkened homes of men;
And the Master whom I love so—
He would say unto me then:
Thou hast in the Master's service
Ever faithful been.
There is work that's always waiting
For the willing hand to do;
In the service of the Master
There is special work for you;
If you love Him, seek and find it—
Maybe at your very door
You will find the mission waiting
That you best are fitted for.
For this kind and loving Master
Let us do the best we can,
Sharing one another's burdens—
Helping on our fellowman.
When I stand before the Master,
May these words His verdict be:
"All the good you did to others,
Even so was done to Me."

J. M. HENSON, 1916

RIALS

In spite of trials I must face, I thank You for being so wonderful, my God. You are the Father in whom I can confide and to whom I go for guidance. You are my Rescuer when I desperately need Your help. Not only did You give Your Son to die for me, You are merciful and loving to me every day. Thank You that Your Spirit dwells within me, comforting and strengthening me though trials and hardships.

I don't know why I must go through these adversities. Is it partly so I can better understand others who need sympathy and encouragement? Will I be able to show them where my help comes from? I praise and thank You, for I know my help comes from You, my God.

Praising You during these trials is extremely difficult for me, especially when I can't see the whys or how longs. This is when I learn to keep my thoughts and heart fixed squarely on You, my God, focusing on what You are trying to show me. Is Your will being revealed through all of this? Is there a purpose?

In spite of these trials, I know I must give thanks in every situation. Your will has first place in my life. You care about what happens to me.

I realize we aren't always promised a life of ease. So in the midst of these trials, I commit them to You, again and again.

I refuse to call them trials any longer. Instead, they are trials turned inside out, transformed into triumphs!

You have promised me in Your Word that wonderful joy awaits me, in spite of the difficulties right now. Are You testing me, Father? Will my faith prove worthy of glorifying You so others may see Your good works? I'm not very strong, but You are here to hold me up when I weaken.

Thank You for teaching me Your priceless lessons while I cling closely to You. Thank You for the skimming of my faults so I may shine forth as purest gold and reflect Your image.

I praise You for helping me submit to Your will through life's fiery trials. Thank You that through Your grace and power You are able to bring out the best and heal the worst in me.

I love You, Lord. I will try to do what is right with all my might and not fail You. As we pass through these trials together to victory triumphant, I will praise and glorify You with all my heart.

Loss

Father, how I praise You for being with me in my loss. Thank You for Your comforting strength. This great loss I am going through is devastating. The very thought overwhelms me and breaks my heart.

"Why me?" I ask. Yet through it all, You understand my troubled soul. I have no answers. I throw all the questions at Your feet, trusting You to help.

Thank You for helping me not be afraid. Though the waters are deep and swift, You do not let me be swept away and drowned. Though attacking fires of stress surround me, and the smoke of uncertainties burns my eyes, I still focus on You, my Lord. You are my God, my Redeemer.

Even when walking through the valley of the shadow of death, I will not be afraid, because You are close to me, watching out for me and showing the way.

You, Emmanuel, are with me. I take comfort and strength in that. How grateful I am for each time You help me not strike out at those around me because of my pain.

In spite of my loss and pain, I thank You for the lessons I'm learning through these trials. I praise You already for victories to come and for Your wonderful, comforting presence.

When I cry unto thee, then shall mine enemies turn back: this I know; for God is for me. In God have I put my trust: I will not be afraid what man can do unto me.

PSALM 56: 9, 11 KJV

JESUS AND I

Fighting the battles of life alone,
I suffer many a sore defeat,
Striving so hard, but I cannot win,
And fall before each foe I meet;
Baffled and beaten, for Help I call,
Then we have victory over all,
Jesus and I, Jesus and I, Jesus and I.

Sometimes the sky is o'ercast with clouds,
The light grows dim and I lose heart,
Plans I had cherished all come to naught,
The friends I trusted stand apart;
Then He appears and the dark is gone!
And O the rapture as we walk on!
Jesus and I, Jesus and I, Jesus and I.

And when the night of my weeping comes,
My heart in agony must bleed,
Shaken by grief that can find no words.
So crushed and weak, uncomforted;
Then of His presence I grow aware,
And we together the load can bear,
Jesus and I, Jesus and I, Jesus and I.

I cannot tell what it means to me
To have so dear, so true a Friend,
Counsel and guidance, and rest and joy,
A friendship that will never end!
Walking together along life's way,
Dwelling together in Heav'n for aye,
Jesus and I, Jesus and I, Jesus and I.

SAMUEL W. BEASLEY, 1915

UNEXPECTED BLESSINGS

Unexpected Blessings

Thank You, Lord, for unexpected blessings. Some are dramatic, others seem small or humorous. These blessings bring zest to my life. I treasure their memories through the years.

I'm grateful for how You not only bless in huge, save-the-world crises, but also in our everyday walk with You. For this, Lord, I give You praise.

The smallest blessings often become the greatest treasures.

The Blanky

Our son and daughter-in-law, Dan and Stayci, were one month away from bringing a new member of our family into the world. They needed to attend an important business function in Portland, about 150 miles away. Doctors advised them not to go, but being young like we all were once, they went anyway.

At the same time, Dad and I were planning a trip to California to see another son. I had already laid aside a special little packet I intended to give Dan and Stayci a month later: a stuffed animal for our older grandson, Harrison; some special things for Stayci; a stuffed animal for our new grand-baby. Along with it I tucked in an outfit Dan wore when he was a baby, his silky blanky filled with countless holes, and his stuffed Tony the Tiger from when he was two.

Just before Dad and I were to leave, we received a call from Portland. The new baby, Riley, had arrived early. We decided to go by way of the hospital, so we headed south to meet Riley for the first time. At the last minute, I stuck the baby packet of goods in my suitcase. We picked up Stayci's mom and were on our way. She would stay with Stayci at a friend's house in Portland for a few days after leaving the hospital.

When we arrived, we found Mommy tired but not appearing too bad after it all. Dan looked like he had been dragged through a knothole. Our new little Riley was hooked up to all sorts of wires like a miniature bionic man. Doctors and nurses said, however, that mother and baby were doing fine. We weren't too sure about the father. Dan paced the room, with cell phone in one hand and a notebook in the other, trying to handle responsibilities at home with Harrison, and the others at the hospital with a dear wife and new baby.

We finally settled around Stayci's hospital bed for a short visit. A charming nurse from the Philippines bustled in and out attentively. Quick snapshots were taken. Then I thought of the baby packet.

I gave Stayci her gifts and handed the bag to Dan. First came the stuffed animals for Harrison and the new baby. Mommy and Daddy seemed pleased. Dan reached in the bag and pulled out his holey blanky.

"My blanky!" he squealed. "This is my blanky, Stayci. I dragged it everywhere. I even held onto it when Mom had it hanging on the clothesline."

Stayci laughed. The nurse rolled her eyes.

Dan reached in again. "Tony the Tiger?" He hugged Tony to him. "Dad and Mom gave him to me when I was two, sick with pneumonia."

Dad was leaning back with an amused grin. Stayci was taking it all in.

"These Americans. . . ," the nurse mumbled with a half grin and shook her head.

We all sat and visited a little longer. Dan and Stayci both appeared more relaxed. Dan began talking about the exciting events over the past couple of days.

I happened to glance down at Dan's hands. The blanky still lay in his lap. His forefinger and thumb absentmindedly rubbed the old, soft, holey blanket, unknowingly soothing him as it had done many years before.

We had prayer together, hugged good-bye, then Dad and I left for California. As we drove away, I wondered to myself what kind of plan God had when I remembered to toss in the silly little baby packet. I paused and silently thanked Him for it.

C. J. AND THE CAT

Ten-year-old C. J. had been in my Sunday school class for two years. I knew him well. One Sunday morning he shared a prayer request with us. He wanted prayer for his sick cat. I lightheartedly added the request to several others as we prayed.

The next Sunday C. J. told how his cat was getting worse and the veterinarian was concerned about the cat's recovery.

It came time for morning worship service. When my husband, Bob, asked for prayer requests, C. J. raised his hand and asked for prayer for his cat.

Bob looked surprised. Some people smiled. Others stifled chuckles. Bob gingerly added C. J.'s request to several others, asking that God would be with C. J.

After church, C. J. came to me. "I want us to pray for my cat, not me," he announced.

At that moment, God spoke to my heart. The two of us sat on the back pew in the sanctuary and prayed earnestly for God to heal C. J.'s cat. Then I turned to my dear student and told him to tell everyone he had prayed for his cat and to give God the praise.

What am I saying? I wondered. *Lord, this is really putting our prayers to the test.*

The next week in Sunday school class C. J. said the cat was recovering. Our class thanked God together.

Later that day, I praised God again for the unexpected little blessing of C. J. and his cat.

MOTHER AND FRIEND

It was Mother's Day. I didn't know how to react. I felt blue because all my grown children were out of town and I wouldn't be able to see them. I knew they would call, but that wouldn't be the same.

The time came for morning church service. Soon after the service began, I felt a long, lanky body slip in beside me on the church pew. Our son, Dave. A warm feeling filled my heart. He was able to make it at the last minute. We had a good time of worship and left afterward for a nearby restaurant.

As we drove down the road, Dave pulled out a package. It contained a picture frame with a hand-written message from my son:

MY MOTHER AND FRIEND

She's one of the strongest people I know.
Her sense of humor will brighten
the darkest of moments,
While she never fails to address
any necessary seriousness.

She looks for good in people
and is persistent about finding it.
She has relentless faith.
She knows how to make
a great bowl of gelatin salad.

She's a writer.
Writes like a madman, up at all hours.
Her typed-out words inspire people,
including me.

We're the same in our sensitivity.
We attempted to go fishing one time,
but neither of us wanted to kill the worm by putting
it on the hook.
Hey, we tried. . .

She treats everyone the same, kindly.
She'll always make time to listen.
She'll always speak her mind.
As her success builds, I'm proud of her,
my mother and friend.
With love, Dave Donihue

What more blessing could I ask? I thank God for
a day I shall never forget.

A Sunday afternoon all to ourselves? Bob and I couldn't believe it.

"Get in the car," he gently prodded.

"Where are we going? Do I look all right?" I glanced at my slacks and top.

I had learned after thirty-eight years of marriage that I had a husband who was filled with romantic surprises. We'd both carried heavy schedules lately and were due for a break.

He opened the door. I climbed in the car. He ran around to the driver's side like a chivalrous twenty year old. We were on our way.

We drove and drove through beautiful countryside. On we went, up over the pass.

"Let's go a little farther," Bob suggested with a gleam in his eyes.

We happily chatted about recent events. We were so caught up in the moment that we missed the turn to return home.

We glanced at each other with adventurous looks. "Let's keep going," we both said at once.

After hours of driving we came to a forest fire and watched the helicopters successfully smother it. We kept driving and passed deer, leisurely munching grass by the side of the road.

Soon we arrived in a small town on the other side of the pass. We had no luggage, toiletries, or changes of clothing. It didn't discourage us. We stopped for the essentials at a nearby grocery store.

We checked into a motel and called our oldest son so no one would think we had disappeared forever. A relaxing night was spent talking and reading.

The next morning we returned home well-rested. We both found we had added another very special memory to our married lives.

I'm thankful for God's plan for relaxation and for my loving husband who knows when we need a break.

COUNT YOUR BLESSINGS

Count your blessings,
Name them one by one;
Count your blessings,
See what God hath done;
Count your blessings,
Name them one by one;
Count your many blessings,
See what God hath done.

To You, Father, I offer my sacrifice—an offering of praise. Strange. It doesn't seem to be a sacrifice, but a fulfillment of my life with You.

I honor You, Father. I thank You and sing praises to You above all else. Each morning I rise with praises on my lips, thanking You for Your lovingkindness. Each evening I thank You for being with me through the day.

I give You everything in my life—the good in me; the faults—so You can help me change. Let me be a living praise to You, dear Lord. May my attitude and motives laud and honor You. May my life be the kind that is acceptable in Your sight. In light of all You have done for me, this seems so little in return.

You sacrificed Your Son. He suffered and died outside Jerusalem where His blood spilled and washed my sins away. Because of this, I will continually offer my sacrifice of praise to You, dear Lord. I will tell everyone who listens about Your glory and love. I will give thanks for all things to You, God the Father, in the name of Your Son, Jesus Christ.

You are worthy of all praise. Worthy to receive power, glory, honor, and adoration beyond limit.

Praise be to You, O God!

Praise ye the LORD.
Praise God in his sanctuary:
praise him in the firmament of his power.

Praise him for his mighty acts;
praise him according to his excellent greatness.

Praise him with the sound of the trumpet:
praise him with the psaltery and harp.

Praise him with the timbrel and dance:
praise him with stringed instruments and organs.

Praise him upon the loud cymbals:
praise him upon the high sounding cymbals.

Let every thing that hath breath
praise the LORD.
Praise ye the LORD.

PSALM 150 KJV

"PRAISE WORKS"

I have a pair of praying hands
A friend once gave to me.
Beside them is the motto:
Praise works, for all to see.

When I am gazing at those hands,
I think of all You've done.
I lift my praise with grateful heart,
And You and I are one.

"Praise works," I hear You telling me
As I dress for the day.
Each duty You will guide me through;
Each toil, You'll show the way.

I do not know what each day holds,
I do know One who's there.
No matter what, I'll still recall,
Praise works, in simple prayer.

Stress and pressures still will come,
With weight beyond degree.
Yet I will keep my thoughts on You,
And praises lift to Thee.

When I begin my projects,
My motto shines out clear:
"Praise works." You whisper tenderly,
"My strength for you is here."

As I'm about to leave my home,
To face another day,
"Praise works," I hear You say again.
I pause. I kneel. I pray.

In those kneeling moments
I lift my praise once more.
I give You my decisions,
And then step through the door.

Returning at the end of day
I think of praise again.
I thank You for the things You've done;
My Savior and my Friend.

MORE INSPIRATION
FOR A WOMAN'S HEART

Also Available from
Barbour Publishing, Inc.

Available wherever books
are sold.